W9-CPO-660

At Issue

What Is a Hate Crime?

Other Books in the At Issue series:

At Issue

| What Is a Hate Crime?

Robert Winters, Book Editor

GREENHAVEN PRESS

An imprint of Thomson Gale, a part of The Thomson Corporation

Detroit • New York • San Francisco • New Haven, Conn. • Waterville, Maine • London

Christine Nasso, *Publisher*
Elizabeth Des Chenes, *Managing Editor*

© 2007 Thomson Gale, a part of The Thomson Corporation.

Thomson and Star logo are trademarks and Gale and Greenhaven Press are registered trademarks used herein under license.

For more information, contact:
Greenhaven Press
27500 Drake Rd.
Farmington Hills, MI 48331-3535
Or you can visit our Internet site at http://www.gale.com

Cover photograph reproduced by permission of Gstar.

LIBRARY OF CONGRESS CATALOGING-IN-PUBLICATION DATA

What is a hate crime? / Robert Winters, book editor.
    p. cm. -- (At issue)
Includes bibliographical references and index.
ISBN-13: 978-0-7377-2436-3 (hardcover)
ISBN-13: 978-0-7377-2437-0 (pbk.)
1. Hate Crimes--Juvenile literature. I. Winters, Robert 1963-
HV6773.5.W478 2007
364.15--dc22
                                                              2007004505

ISBN-10: 0-7377-2436-6 (hardcover)
ISBN-10: 0-7377-2437-4 (pbk.)

Printed in the United States of America
10 9 8 7 6 5 4 3 2 1

Contents

Introduction

The term "hate crime" is a bit of a misnomer. There are many crimes motivated by deeply personal hatreds, of an abusive spouse, a nasty and violent neighbor, a child's murderer, a cheating mate. These are not hate crimes. Hate crimes instead are oddly impersonal. The victim is chosen not because of what he or she has done or might do to the perpetrator. They are chosen because they share some characteristic with a larger group that enrages the perpetrator for reasons that may have nothing to do with the actual victim.

There is a sharp divide on how to treat these types of crimes.

On one side, there are those who say, "Punish acts, not thoughts." After all, this has been the position of the law for centuries. Proving motive may be necessary for conviction, but then it is the crime itself which is punished, in this view. Or maybe not. Actually, motive often enters into punishment. Almost everyone, including judges, recognizes the difference between killing somebody to save the life of another and killing somebody to keep them from reporting a robbery. For most, there is a profound difference between killing a terminally ill parent to end their suffering and killing the same parent to get an inheritance faster, although both may be punishable.

Still, in many cases, motive does not matter. Embezzling to pay the rent and embezzling to buy a video game player may receive exactly the same sentence. It is quite possible for a jury and a judge to be completely indifferent toward a bank robber's motivation. The fact that he clearly threatened to kill a teller and took the money may be the only consideration. A drunken bar fight, punching out a roommate in an unusually violent fight, attacking a hated supervisor at work can all carry exactly the same sentence for the exact same crime: assault and battery.

For most states and the federal government, the wider motive is very much a consideration in hate crimes. They are seen as assaults on vital, widely shared social ideals as well as assaults on a particular victim. If somebody beats up a random African American as a warning to all African Americans to stay out of an area, that is an assault on the very idea of integration and freedom of mobility and assembly. Desecrating a Jewish cemetery with swastikas is a fairly clear statement that Jews are unwelcome and they should be afraid. For many, it is simply common sense for the larger society to recognize this and treat these crimes as worse than simple assault or vandalism.

Others disagree sharply, citing the First Amendment and the founding ideals of this government. This is not a country that mandates shared opinions. Whatever government says, whatever the majority of Americans might like, racism, anti-Semitism, misogyny, and a whole range of bigotries are legal and constitutionally protected. That does not mean everyone is free to act on those bigotries however they see fit, but government can never go beyond punishing those acts into punishing the ideas behind them. That puts government in the tyrannical position of deciding what ideas are legal and what are not, which thoughts are valid or at least acceptable and which must be punished more severely.

Then there is the question of application. Even if hate crime laws are legitimate in theory, they are limited to certain types of groups. Gender, race, ethnicity, and religion are generally accepted as protected categories by hate crimes advocates and legislatures. But sexual orientation often is not. It is undeniable that people are assaulted and even killed because they are gay or perceived to be gay, although the extent of these crimes and whether the problem is getting worse or better is actively debated. Still, many virulently resist including sexual orientation in hate crime statutes, even if they accept the idea of hate crimes legislation itself. For them, this inclusion amounts to an official declaration that homosexuality is innate, not chosen, normal rather than deviant, and just as acceptable as racial and religious difference. They deny all these propositions, and some even go so far as to define these ideas as a kind of hate crime against Christian fundamentalists. Others see it as ridiculous that crimes obviously motivated by hatred of gay people must not be treated that way for fear of offending people's religious beliefs.

Finally there is the even more controversial matter of hate speech. Hate crimes imply an underlying, clearly recognized crime, from simple vandalism to brutal murder. Hate speech codes go further and seek to punish words that may lead to crimes or that may amount to an assault in the minds of the victims. Aside from the threats to free speech there is a very real question as to what kind of speech actually constitutes hate speech, as opposed to sharp disagreement or disapproval.

The same of course can be said about determining whether group hatred is a true motivator behind a particular crime and a particular victim. Still, hate crime laws seem to be here to stay, in federal law and the laws of most states. Students, voters, and jurors can all benefit from a greater understanding of what makes hate crimes different, the reasons for enacting hate crime legislation, and the challenges they raise.

1

Hate Crimes Are Not Like Other Crimes

Nancy Turner

Nancy Turner is the senior program manager for the International Association of Chiefs of Police and has served as a victims' advocate and activist against violence directed at women since 1985. She is also a faculty member in George Washington University's Women's Studies program.

Although specific laws vary across different jurisdictions, hate crimes are distinct from other criminal offenses. They are motivated by bias against the victim's perceived race, gender, sexual orientation, religion, or ethnicity. Because of that, they are often more brutal than other crimes and also have ripple effects, spreading fear throughout entire communities. Unlike hate incidents, hate crimes are actual criminal offenses, such as assault or vandalism, rather than hostile speech or other behavior that is legally protected, however biased. They also depend to an unusual degree on victims' perceptions and cooperation, which make it imperative that police exercise sensitivity and a lack of prejudice in their investigations.

A hate crime is a criminal offense committed against persons, property or society that is motivated, in whole or in part, by an offender's bias against an individual's or a group's race, religion, ethnic/national origin, gender, age, disability or sexual orientation. (Definition developed at the 1998 IACP [International Association of Chiefs of Police] Summit on Hate Crime in America.)

Nancy Turner, "Responding to Hate Crimes: A Police Officer's Guide to Investigation and Prevention," *IACP*, December 7, 2001. Reproduced by permission.

Legal definitions of hate crimes vary. The federal definition of hate crimes addresses civil rights violations under 18 U.S.C. Section 245.

As of 1999, 41 states and the District of Columbia have hate crime statutes that provide enhanced penalties for crimes in which victims are selected because of a perpetrator's bias against a victim's perceived race, religion or ethnicity. Many states also classify as hate crimes those in which a victim is selected based on a perception of his/her sexual orientation.

Hate crime definitions often encompass not only violence against individuals or groups but also crimes against property, such as arson or vandalism, particularly those directed against community centers or houses of worship. Check your state statutes for the definition of hate crime in your jurisdiction.

Accurate and comprehensive police reporting is essential to understanding the prevalence and patterns of hate crimes both locally and nationally.

The federal Hate Crimes Statistics Act of 1990 (Public Law 102-275 April 23, 1990) encourages states to report hate crime data to the Federal Bureau of Investigation (FBI). Twenty-three states and the District of Columbia require the collection of hate crime data. In 1997, 11,211 state and local law enforcement agencies voluntarily reported 9,861 hate crime offenses to the FBI.

Elements of Hate Crimes

Hate crimes differ from other crimes in their effect on victims and on community stability:

- Hate crimes are often especially brutal or injurious.

- Victim(s) usually feel traumatized and terrified.

- Families of victims often feel frustrated and powerless.

- Others in the community who share the victim's characteristics may feel victimized and vulnerable.

- Hate incidents can escalate and prompt retaliatory action.

- Hate crimes and hate incidents create communitywide unrest. A swift and strong response by law enforcement can help stabilize and calm the community as well as aid in a victim's recovery. Failure to respond to hate crimes within departmental guidelines may jeopardize public safety and leave officers and departments open to increased scrutiny and possible liability.

It is the perpetrator's perception of difference (whether accurate or not) motivating his or her criminal behavior that would constitute a hate crime.

The Difference Between a Hate Incident and a Hate Crime

Hate incidents involve behaviors that, though motivated by bias against a victim's race, religion, ethnic/national origin, gender, age, disability or sexual orientation, are not criminal acts. Hostile or hateful speech, or other disrespectful/discriminatory behavior may be motivated by bias but is not illegal. They become crimes only when they directly incite perpetrators to commit violence against persons or property, or if they place a potential victim in reasonable fear of physical injury. Officers should thoroughly document evidence in all bias-motivated incidents. Law enforcement can help to defuse potentially dangerous situations and prevent bias-motivated criminal behavior by responding to and documenting bias-motivated speech or behavior even if it does not rise to the level of a criminal offense. . . .

Differences from Other Crimes

The main difference between a hate crime and other crimes is that a perpetrator of a hate crime is motivated by bias. To evaluate a perpetrator's motives, you should consider several bias indicators:

- perceptions of the victim(s) and witnesses about the crime

- the perpetrator's comments, gestures or written statements that reflect bias, including graffiti or other symbols

- any differences between perpetrator and victim, whether actual or perceived by the perpetrator

- similar incidents in the same location or neighborhood to determine whether a pattern exists

- whether the victim was engaged in activities promoting his/her group or community—for example, by clothing or conduct

- whether the incident coincided with a holiday or [date] of particular significance

- involvement of organized hate groups or their members

- absence of any other motive such as economic gain The presence of any of these factors does not confirm that the incident was a hate offense but may indicate the need for further investigation into motive.

Victims' Perspective

A victim's perception is an important factor to consider, but be aware that victims may not recognize the crime as motivated by bias. Victims should not be asked directly whether they believe they were the victim of a hate crime, but it is appropriate to ask if they have any idea why they might have been victimized.

Victims and perpetrators may appear to be from the same race, ethnicity/nationality, or religion, but it is the perpetrator's perception of difference (whether accurate or not) motivating his or her criminal behavior that would constitute a hate crime.

Hate crimes are unique. Victims of hate crimes are targeted because of a core characteristic of their identity. These attributes cannot be changed. Victims often feel degraded, frightened, vulnerable and suspicious. This may be one of the most traumatic experiences of the[ir] lives. Community members who share with victims the characteristics that made them targets of hate (race, religion, ethnic/national origin, gender, age, disability or sexual orientation) may also feel vulnerable, fearful and powerless. In this emotional atmosphere, law enforcement officers and investigators must attend carefully to the ways they interact and communicate with victims, their families and members of the community.

2

The Growth of Hate Crimes Legislation

Phyllis B. Gerstenfeld

An associate professor of criminal justice at California State University, Stanislaus, Phyllis B. Gerstenfeld has specialized in study of hate crimes legislation. She is the author of Hate Crimes: Causes, Controls, and Controversies *and* Crimes of Hate: Selected Readings.

In 1977, a neo-Nazi group attempted to hold a rally in Skokie, Illinois, which had a large Jewish population including many Holocaust survivors. Outraged, the Anti-Defamation League began to monitor anti-Semitic incidents throughout the country, which seemed to be increasing at an alarming rate. Joining with other groups fighting prejudice against black people and gays and lesbians, the ADL devised model legislation against hate crimes, including provisions for enhanced penalties and for victims to sue their attackers for bias. As of 2000, all but seven states have adopted hate crimes legislation, many based on the ADL model. The federal government has also adopted some hate crimes legislation, though more narrowly tailored. In addition a number of communities and college campuses have adopted hate speech codes, which do not depend on any underlying crime and have proved considerably more controversial.

In 1977, a neo-Nazi group called the National Socialist Party of America (NSPA) wished to hold a demonstration in front of the village hall in Skokie, Illinois. Skokie had a large Jewish population, many of whom were Holocaust survivors. The village first obtained an injunction against the event and then passed a series of ordinances that would have prohibited the NSPA from obtaining the necessary permits. The NSPA sued (with the assistance of the American Civil Liberties Union), and eventually won the right to demonstrate. Although the NSPA ultimately never did march in Skokie, the controversy received national attention, even to the extent of being satirized in the movie *The Blues Brothers.*

One organization that paid special attention was the Anti-Defamation League of B'nai B'rith (ADL), a group that combats anti-Semitism and other forms of bigotry. Beginning in 1978, the ADL started tracking anti-Semitic incidents across the United States. Between 1978 and 1981, the number of reported incidents increased from 49 to 974. Alarmed by what it interpreted as a disturbing trend, and frustrated with existing federal and state laws, the ADL drafted a model ethnic intimidation statute in 1981. Together with allies such as the National Gay and Lesbian Task Force, the National Institute for Prejudice and Violence, and the Southern Poverty Law Center, the ADL began lobbying states to pass the statute.

When it was passed, the model statute contained four provisions. The first of these, Institutional Vandalism, was aimed primarily at people who targeted cemeteries, community centers, and places of worship. It was not a new idea, as some states already had similar laws on the books, but the ADL and its allies clearly wanted more states to follow suit.

The second provision was more revolutionary. Although it was likely inspired by existing civil rights laws, it was quite different in scope. Under this provision, a person would be found guilty of an "intimidation" if he or she violated some existing criminal law, and if he or she committed the crime because of the victim's group (or perceived group). Although only certain types of groups were protected—race, color, religion, national origin, and sexual orientation—this was a significant expansion upon civil rights laws. The model statute also specified that it would act as a penalty enhancer, essentially bumping up the seriousness of the underlying crime by one degree. Thus, someone who committed what ordinarily would have been a Class C Felony, for example, could now be sentenced for a Class B Felony.

The ADL later modified this section of the model statute slightly. It renamed it "Bias-Motivated Crimes," and it also added gender to the list of protected groups. The substance, however, remained the same.

The third provision of the model statute creates a civil cause of action so that victims of institutional vandalism and bias crimes may sue their attackers. Antihate groups have found civil actions to be a particularly useful strategy. . . .

Finally, the model statute provides for collection of law enforcement data on bias crimes and for specialized training of police officers.

State Laws

The ADL's efforts to persuade states to pass hate crime legislation were successful. Very soon after the ADL drafted the model statute in 1981, a few states, such as Oregon and Washington, passed similar laws. Other states quickly followed suit. By 1994, 34 states and the District of Columbia had some kind of penalty-enhancement–type law and, by 2000, only seven states did not.

Only one state—Wyoming—has no hate crime provisions at all.

Although many of the states used the ADL model as a guide, they frequently made substantial changes when they first passed their laws, as well as in subsequent amendments. Other states created their statutes from scratch rather than using the model. As a result, existing hate crime legislation today is quite diverse. Some laws act as pure penalty enhancers, increasing the sentence for crimes motivated by bias. The increase can be substantial: In some situations, the maximum sentence may be doubled, tripled, or increased by even more. These laws can also result in misdemeanors being reclassified as felonies, which can have serious legal implications for the offender. Other states created a separate substantive offense, for which the offender may be convicted in addition to receiving a conviction for the underlying crime. In any of these cases, the practical effect is that the defendant faces more severe penalties than he or she would for an ordinary crime.

There are other differences between the states as well. Some permit any underlying crime to qualify as a hate crime, whereas some limit their definition to certain specific offenses, such as harassment, assault, and vandalism. Some include language that the victim must have been chosen "because of" or "by reason" of his or her group, whereas others simply require that the crime "evidence" or "demonstrate" prejudice or that prejudice be "manifest." The states also differ substantially as to which groups are enumerated in the statute. All statutes include at least race, religion, and ethnicity (or national origin), but only 23 include sexual orientation, 21 include gender, 23 include mental or physical disability, 4 include political affiliation, and 4 include age. . . .

Finally, in addition to the penalty-enhancement–type laws, some states also have additional, related laws. Most (40 states) have laws prohibiting institutional vandalism. Almost half (24 states) have statutes regarding collection of hate crime data. A few (10 states) have laws relating to specialized training for law enforcement personnel. And many (28 states) also authorize civil actions. A handful of states—California, Illinois, Louisiana, Massachusetts, Minnesota, and Washington—have all five types of laws. Only one state—Wyoming—has no hate crime provisions at all.

Federal Hate Crime Statutes

Having experienced success in their lobbying efforts with the states, the ADL and its allies turned to the federal government. The gains there, although still substantial, were slower and more qualified.

The first federal law relating specifically to hate crimes was enacted in 1990. Called the Hate Crimes Statistics Act (HCSA), it required the United States Department of Justice to collect data on hate crimes from local law enforcement agencies and to publish the results. The law itself was very strongly supported in Congress. Only four senators voted against it, all on the basis that it included sexual orientation within its enumerated categories. Although the HCSA was originally set to expire in 1995, it was later extended through fiscal year 2002. . . .

In 1994, Congress passed the Hate Crimes Sentencing Enhancement Act. This law essentially acted as a federal penalty enhancement statute. It ordered the United States Sentencing Commission to revise sentencing requirements for situations where a person was being tried for a federal crime, and where the defendant intentionally selected the victim because of the victim's group. The penalty was to be increased at least three levels. It is important to note that this law is of limited potential scope because, as we have already discussed, federal criminal prosecutions are relatively rare, at least in comparison with state prosecutions. . . .

Also in 1994, Congress passed the Violence Against Women Act (VAWA). Among other things, this law provided that victims of gender-based crimes could sue their attackers and receive compensatory and punitive damages. This law could be seen as an extension of existing hate crimes legislation, none of which included gender. However, as already mentioned, the Supreme Court declared a portion of VAWA unconstitutional in 2000 because it exceeded Congress's authority under the Commerce Clause.

Another specialized federal hate crime law is the Church Arson Prevention Act, passed unanimously in 1997. This law was a reaction to a reported spike in the numbers of church burnings in the mid-1990s; many of the affected churches had predominantly African American congregations. The law contains a number of provisions, including facilitating federal prosecutions and increasing penalties for damaging places of worship.

One additional piece of federal legislation, the Hate Crimes Prevention Act, has been bouncing around Congress for several years now. It was originally proposed in 1998 but was then put aside as Congress became busy with the impeachment hearings of then President [William] Clinton. In 1999, two competing bills were introduced by Senators [Edward] Kennedy and [Orrin] Hatch. Both would have extended federal jurisdiction in hate crime cases. The primary difference between them was that Kennedy's bill included crimes based on sexual orientation, whereas Hatch's did not. Both bills died in committee. Kennedy's bill was revised and reintroduced in 2001 as the Local Law Enforcement Enhancement Act; in early 2002, the bill was once again killed in committee.

The debates about hate speech codes were, to say the least, lively.

Hate Speech

All of the laws that we have discussed in this chapter assume that the offenders commit some underlying criminal act. But what if they do not? What if, for example, I want to display a swastika on my own property, or call someone else a racially disparaging name? Can I be punished for that?

A general definition of hate speech is words or symbols that are derogatory or offensive on the basis of race, religion, sexual orientation, and so on. The critical distinction between hate *crime* and hate *speech* is that the former requires some underlying criminal act; the latter does not. In the case of hate speech, it is the speech itself that is punished.

Many commentators have argued that hate speech is dangerous and harmful. According to these people, not only does hate speech have many of the same effects as hate crimes (psychological trauma, adverse impact on the community, etc.), but it also may foster an atmosphere in which bias-motivated violence is encouraged, subtly or explicitly.

As a result of these arguments, many college campuses created codes prohibiting certain kinds of speech. These codes varied widely in scope and quality; some were so broadly written as to encompass a great deal of legitimate academic discourse. Critics claimed that not only were these codes a violation of the First Amendment freedom of speech, but also that they interfered with academic freedom and hobbled scholarship and the exchange of ideas.

Hate speech restrictions were created in a few other situations as well. For example, St. Paul, Minnesota, enacted a city ordinance that prohibited offensive symbols or displays in public places.

The debates about hate speech codes were, to say the least, lively. Eventually, of course, these debates entered the legal arena. In cases in Michigan and Wisconsin, federal courts struck down campus speech codes as impermissible restrictions on freedom of speech. In 1992, the United States Supreme Court entered the fray when it decided the case of *R.A.V. v. City of St. Paul.* In that case, the Court held that St. Paul's ordinance was unconstitutional. . . . A year later, the Court held that hate *crime* laws are permissible. Thus, the distinction between hate speech and hate crime is extremely important: One cannot be punished, and the other can.

As you might imagine, the line between hate crime and hate speech is often quite thin. Laypeople quite frequently use the terms interchangeably. Perhaps the simplest way to distinguish them is to ask whether the perpetrator has violated any other criminal law. If I trespass onto your property and burn a cross, that is a hate crime. If I burn the cross on my own property (assuming I have not violated any burning ordinances or the like), that is hate speech.

Often, the distinction between hate crime and hate speech is as simple as the distinction between conduct and expression. Hate crime and hate speech become especially hard to tell apart in two situations: verbal acts and symbolic expression. A verbal act occurs when words themselves constitute some element of a crime. For example, a person can be convicted of the crimes of harassment or making terroristic threats based solely on the words he or she has spoken or written. This is not a violation of freedom of speech. The problem comes when we try to distinguish general statements of rancor, which may be distasteful but which are protected, from actual threats, which are not protected. If I say, "I hate you and I wish you would die," that is probably okay; if I say, "I hate you and I'm going to kill you," I can go to prison.

The second problematic situation occurs when a person does not say a word, and yet still expresses a thought or idea. The Supreme Court calls this symbolic expression or expressive conduct. In a series of cases over the last four decades, the Court has held that actions such as burning a flag or wearing a black armband express ideas, and therefore are protected by the first amendment. In *R.A.V.*, the Court held that cross-burning fell in this category. On the other hand, the Court has also stated that actions such as burning a draft card and dancing nude were merely conduct, and not protected. Clearly, it can sometimes be difficult to classify speech and conduct.

Entire books could be . . . written on the subject of hate speech alone. Because the issues involved are significantly different from those involved with hate crimes, we will leave a more involved discussion of hate speech for other venues.

Conclusion

Although laws addressing some bias-related acts have existed since the Civil War, hate crime legislation as such is a modern phenomenon. Over the past two decades, it has sprung up rather quickly in most states, as well as within the federal codes. Furthermore, there is good reason to believe that hate crime laws will continue to evolve in the near future.

The need for special hate crime laws has been asserted by many people and has been supported by a number of cogent and rational arguments. What remains missing, for the most part, is empirical evidence to substantiate those arguments. Of course, some might argue, such empirical evidence is not really necessary; even if the laws are not particularly required, they can do little harm.

3

Hate Crimes Deserve Harsher Punishment

Christopher Heath Wellman

Christopher Heath Wellman is an associate professor of philosophy at Washington University in St. Louis. He is the author of A Theory of Secession: The Case for Political Self-Determination *(2005) and* For and Against: Is There a Duty to Obey the Law? *(2005).*

It might seem that adding extra penalties for hate crimes is unfair. However, examining the major philosophical schools of thought about punishment of crimes shows this is not so. There are many justifications for punishing criminals, ranging from the practical to the purely moral, and they might all vary in their view of adding stiffer penalties for crimes motivated by hate. Nevertheless, they all justify the application of hate crime laws, one way or another.

Whether it is legitimate to enhance penalties for hate crimes presumably depends upon what justifies state punishment in general, but this raises complications because ordinary moral thinking includes a miscellany [variety] of intuitions regarding punishment, and none of the traditional theories seems able to accommodate all of them. Thankfully, the limited purposes of this essay do not require us to adjudicate definitively among these rival accounts because proponents of each can make a case for stiffer penalties. With this

Christopher Heath Wellman, "A Defense of Stiffer Penalties for Hate Crimes," *Hypatia: A Journal of Feminist Philosophy*, vol. 21, spring 2006. Copyright Indiana University Press Spring 2006. Reproduced by permission of Indiana University Press.

in mind, I will quickly explain each of the theories and then show why all are compatible with punishing bias criminals more strenuously.

The philosophical literature on punishment is replete with various accounts that defy easy categorization, so any clean taxonomy [classification system] will necessarily be somewhat arbitrary and insensitive to the subtleties of existing theories. With this disclaimer, I shall divide what I take to be the most prominent options according to their general justifying aims. I label these theories the Retributive, Utilitarian, Moral Education, Expressivist, Restitutive, and Societal Safety-Valve accounts of punishment. Consider each in turn.

According to retributivism, the general justifying aim of punishment is to serve justice: Criminals should be punished, quite apart from whatever consequences might result, simply because they deserve it. Justice demands that people get what they deserve, criminals deserve to be punished, and so we serve justice when we criminally punish wrongdoers. Retributivism is backward looking insofar as its exclusive concern is to ensure that people receive their just deserts for past conduct. In fixing the appropriate punishment, the retributivist will ignore future consequences and mete out a sentence that fits the gravity of the offense.

Utilitarian Argument

According to utilitarians, retributivists are wrong to look backward since acts, practices, and institutions are to be morally evaluated in terms of their consequences. Thus, if punishing criminals is morally justified, it is because such a practice produces a better state of affairs. Moreover, since the hard treatment of criminals is among the consequences that must be counted, there is a prima facie [obvious] case against punishment. It is not difficult for a utilitarian to defeat this case, however, because there are also ample benefits. Most notably, because all of us want to avoid punishment, each of us is deterred from behaving criminally. And, because others are similarly deterred, we enjoy a level of security possible only under a system of criminal punishment. Thus, state punishment can be justified on consequentialist grounds despite the pain visited upon those punished, because it allows us to pursue our projects in a way that we could not in its absence.

According to the moral education view, the general justifying aim of punishment is to educate the criminal and, where possible, the general public as well. Underlying this approach is a conviction that criminal behavior emanates from some type of correctable moral failing, and the purpose of punishment is to morally educate offenders so that they (and others) will know better than to behave criminally. Moreover, whereas a simple spanking might be appropriate for a dog, humans have reason and thus are capable of being persuaded not to repeat their errors. As a consequence, when we punish humans, we should set out rationally to persuade them that they ought to behave otherwise. Having done so, we will not have harmed them; rather, we will have benefited them with a moral education. In the end, then, a properly designed penal system will not be so hard to justify because it will be constructed to benefit not only society as a whole, but especially the criminals themselves.

In "The Expressive Function of Punishment," [published in 1998] Joel Feinberg argued that a satisfactory definition of punishment must account for its expressive function. He wrote, "Punishment is a conventional device for the expression of attitudes of resentment and indignation, and of judgments of disapproval and reprobation, on the part either of the punishing authority himself or of those 'in whose name' the punishment is inflicted. Punishment, in short, has a symbolic significance largely missing from other kinds of penalties." Impressed with this insight, some suppose that the general justifying aim of punishment is for society to issue its official pronouncements as to how citizens ought to behave.

After all, the state does not merely lock criminals up, it typically does so with a rhetorical flourish that allows a society to express and reinforce its values. In a 1949 memorandum submitted as evidence to the British Royal Commission on Capital Punishment, Lord Justice Denning explained the expressivist position: "The ultimate justification for any punishment is, not that it is a deterrent, but that it is the emphatic denunciation by the community of a crime."

Restitutive Theory

According to the restitutive theory of punishment, the ultimate purpose of punishment is to restore the victim. Rather than focus on harming the criminal, advocates of this approach are concerned principally with benefiting the victim. The logic behind this approach is compelling: Criminal behavior involves one person wrongly arrogating herself above another. Thus, crimes leave the criminal unjustly elevated and the victim wrongly degraded. Unlike retributivists (whose chief aim is to harm the criminal so that she no longer enjoys her undeserved, elevated position), restitutivists insist that our concern must be to restore the victim to her rightful, pre-crime position. Punishment is thought to restore the victim by undoing the degradation of the crime. It repairs the victim's position by publicly confirming that the victim has a moral standing that the criminal was wrong to disrespect.

> *The stakes are raised so dramatically with hate crimes because, to the extent that members of the target group identify with the victim, each is personally slighted by the crime.*

Finally, consider the societal safety-valve theory. As its name suggests, this view takes the general justifying aim of state punishment to be the provision of a safe, institutionally controlled release of destructive animosity [hatred] and vio-

27

lent ill will. Behind this theory are the twin beliefs that members of society must have some outlet for their thirst for personal revenge and general rage at wrongdoing and that channeling this emotion through the state's legal system is the most effective, peaceful avenue available. If we left it up to individuals to punish those who trespass against them, for instance, many would be frustrated by their inability to apprehend and punish their assailants, while others would let their lust for revenge lead them either to over-punish or, even worse, to punish innocent people. The innocent who were wrongly punished, the guilty who were over-punished, and even the guilty who falsely supposed that they were over-punished would then retaliate in their own bids for revenge. As these considerations reveal, it would not be long before a system of individual punishments deteriorated into a bloody mess. Because state punishment enjoys the moral authority that can come only through impartially adjudicating conflicts, it offers a relatively peaceful safety valve for the passionate resentment against perceived wrongdoers.

Applying the Theories to Hate Crimes Penalties

In light of this description of the competing accounts, let us consider, in reverse order, whether proponents of each of these approaches could justify harsher punishments for hate criminals. As advocates of the societal safety valve theory emphasize, criminal punishments provide an important outlet for potentially disruptive tensions, especially when the victims have been severely mistreated. Nowhere is this release of societal pressure more important than in cases where divisions within society have led to bias crimes. The stakes are raised so dramatically with hate crimes because, to the extent that members of the target group identify with the victim, each is personally slighted by the crime and thus has much more than an impartial interest in seeing justice done. Thus, whereas only an individual and perhaps her friends and family will be personally invested in an average criminal's penalty, an entire marked group will typically yearn for a hate criminal to receive her just desert [get what she deserves]. The rioting in Los Angeles following the acquittal of the police officers who brutally beat Rodney King was a striking example of this phenomenon. One did not have to be a black person living in southern California to be outraged by the jury's verdict, but blacks were more than dispassionate enemies of injustice, they were fellow travelers who felt personally degraded by the beating and subsequently insulted by the verdict. Given their understandable investment in the court's decision, the acquittal understandably enraged many blacks.

It would be wrong to pretend that this extreme example is generally representative of what will happen if hate criminals are not given stiffer punishments (even the most heinous case is unlikely to be so combustible in the absence of other aggravating factors), but the Rodney King case does illustrate that hate crimes are lamentably capable of ripping the fabric that binds society's distinct groups. As such, it shows why, if at least one of the functions of criminal punishment is to serve as a peaceful outlet for potentially explosive social pressure, the additional socially disruptive element peculiar to bias crimes explains why we should seek stiffer punishments in these cases.

Turning now to the restitutive view, there are two distinct means of support for more severe punishments. Most obviously, one can claim that a hate crime especially degrades its direct victim, and thus calls for a more strenuous punishment to restore the victim to her ex ante [previous, literally "before the event"] position. Although I think it is plausible to suppose that hate crimes are particularly degrading to their primary victims, I will not focus on this claim here. Rather, drawing upon the observations made just above, I suggest that hate crimes require enhanced penalties because, more than other transgressions, hate crimes claim vicarious victims. Each time a person is targeted for assault because of the group to which she belongs, it takes a toll upon everyone in the marked group. This is especially so in a society where members of the group are regularly attacked. Without diminishing the fact that the primary victim is often devastated as no one else could be, I want to stress that others are importantly, if vicariously, made victims because of their identification with the victim and the effect this identification has upon their sense of belonging, and even security, in society. . . .

Thus, even without asserting that hate crimes are especially damaging to their primary victims, one can cite the real losses of secondary victims to explain why the restoration made necessary by hate crimes is more substantial than that by ordinary crimes. Put simply, hate crimes leave so much pain and degradation in their wake that, in order to restore both the primary and secondary victims, society must employ extraordinary measures to affirm all those who have been degraded. In such circumstances, ordinary criminal censure will not do.

The Expressivist Case

Standing upon the shoulders of the preceding two analyses, one can create a compelling expressivist case for stiffer punishments. To do so, it is important to appreciate that one reason hate crimes are so ghastly and troubling is because of the messages they send. As indicated above, a hate crime can serve as a poignant announcement to all members of the targeted group that they are despised, hunted, and vulnerable. Indeed, part of what attracts hate criminals to these horrific acts is the opportunity to express contempt, not just for the particular victim, but for the entire group to which the victim belongs. Unfortunately, this expression is all too often received loud and clear. Proponents of the expressivist theory of punishment are in a position to recognize that hate crimes send these messages and suggest that the criminal law can be used to counter this message. Think again, for instance, of the reaction to the Rodney King episode. Many blacks interpreted the police brutality as a demonstration of the contempt many whites have for them. Given this message, it was especially important that the police officers who were videotaped committing the assault (and then recorded joking about having enjoyed the beating) be publicly censured and punished by society as a whole. If these officers had been criminally sentenced, this legal condemnation would have gone some way toward showing that, while various individuals may be racist, society as a whole will neither condone nor tolerate racist violence. . . . Thus, if the officers had been not only criminally punished but given a more severe sentence for having committed a hate crime, this verdict would have changed the social context surrounding the crime. Such a verdict might have sent a powerful, countervailing [opposing] message that racist violence is emphatically not accepted. Instead, the acquittal only reinforced the message that America as a society condones violence, as long as it is committed by whites against blacks.

In light of the above, it takes little imagination to see why proponents of the expressivist theory of punishment might favor enhanced punishments. Given that the criminal law is an important expression of a society's values, it follows that we should want more severe penalties for those crimes that we deem to be more serious. As the British Royal Commission on Capital Punishment emphasized: "It is essential that punishments inflicted for grave crimes should adequately reflect the revulsion felt by the great majority of citizens for them." And, since we are especially aghast [shocked] at bias crimes, we should want to express our most solemn condemnation for those who commit these crimes. That most natural way for us to do so, of course, is to impose stiffer penalties for hate crimes. As the foregoing discussion illustrates, this general lesson is particularly important in the case of hate crimes because of the destructive and divisive messages they send. Given the implicit but clear messages of bias crimes, it is all the more important that society use criminal law to communicate forcefully that the message of hatred not only does not come from all of us, but is a loathsome message which we as a society will not tolerate.

Applying the Moral Education Theory

In the section below on retributivism, I contend that hate criminals are morally worse than ordinary criminals. If this is accurate, then clearly the moral education theory of punishment would recommend stiffer punishments for hate criminals. Very simply, the type and extent of moral education one requires depends upon the moral depravity of one's character. Thus, if hate criminals are indeed worse than their counterparts, then it stands to reason that they require a more intense moral education. In other words, just as someone guilty of grand larceny merits more severe punishment than a petty thief, a hate criminal should be punished more than someone guilty of an otherwise comparable, generic crime.

But, while this reasoning supplies a compelling case for enhanced penalties, it is not the most pressing concern moral education theorists should have with hate crimes. As critical as it is that we attend to bias criminals after they have violently acted upon their hatred, it is even more important that we strive to become a society in which no one harbors this bias to begin with. This too is a matter of criminal law because, as education theorists emphasize, the criminal code is an important instrument for morally educating society at large. (It can make an enormous difference, for instance, whether one grows up in a society that outlaws homosexuality or in one that doles out more severe penalties to heterosexists who harass homosexuals.) Since chauvinism and xenophobia [hatred of foreigners] are some of the most personally and socially destructive moral vices undermining contemporary society, there are compelling reasons to harness the criminal law's power to shape the general public's values in the campaign against group hatred. In sum, both because hate criminals have revealed themselves to be particularly in need of moral education, and because our criminal code is an educative instrument for society at large, moral education theorists have reason to lobby for enhanced penalties for hate crimes.

The utilitarian case for more strenuous punishments can be mounted on many fronts. In addition to the considerations canvassed above (certainly a utilitarian will want to foster moral education and supply an appropriate societal safety valve, for instance), utilitarians recognize that the optimal punishment is fixed by a number of factors, including the cost of the crime. In short, as the cost of a crime rises, a utilitarian will be more concerned to deter it and will therefore want a more severe punishment. Since hate crimes cause profound social division and unrest, as well as create more pain for a greater number of victims, they are extremely costly. Thus, although a utilitarian might invoke any number of considerations to defend stiffer penalties for hate crimes, one basic and distinctively consequential line of reasoning stands out: the magnified harmfulness of hate crimes gives us reason to attach more severe penalties to those found guilty of committing them.

To most, I suspect that the heightened guilt of the hate criminal's mind seems self-evident.

Finally, because retributivists advocate punishing criminals in accordance with the moral depravity of their offenses, they must establish that hate crimes are worse than their generic counterparts. Corresponding to the two elements of any crime, actus reus (bad act) and mens rea (guilty mind), there are two ways in which bias crimes and criminals might be morally worse than ordinary ones: if the act is worse or the mind more guilty, then there is a retributive case for stiffer penalties.

The explanation as to why the actus reus in a hate crime is particularly bad is straightforward. As outlined above, bias crimes are especially harmful because of the vicarious victims they claim and the psychological distress and social unrest they leave in their wake. And, just as a person who steals one thousand dollars commits a worse act (other things being equal) than someone who steals one hundred, the additional harms involved in bias crimes make the acts worse than they would be otherwise. Clearly, then, proponents of retributivism need cite only the magnified badness of the act in a hate crime to show why bias criminals are especially culpable and thus deserve to be punished more.

An Illustrative Example

If a bias crime's actus reus is particularly bad, then a retributivist need not establish that the mens rea is any different from that in generic crimes. Because I believe that the mind of a hate criminal is especially depraved, however, let me suggest how a retributivist might focus on mens rea to make the case for enhanced punishment. To most, I suspect that the heightened guilt of the hate criminal's mind seems self-evident. If Ally and Barry both murder someone, for instance, and the only difference between the two is that Ally chooses her victim for monetary gain (suppose she is paid ten thousand dollars to kill someone she has never met) whereas Barry is motivated solely by hatred for the group to which his victim belongs (imagine that Barry kills a Jewish woman he has never met only because she is Jewish), most would agree that Barry's offense is worse. As much as Ally ought to be punished, Barry deserves a stiffer punishment to fit his extreme depravity.

For those who do not share this pretheoretic judgment, let me offer a buttressing [supporting] explanation. In my view, Barry's murder is made worse by the additional element of invidious discrimination. The wrongness of invidious discrimination is not mysterious; most everyone understands the appeal of Martin Luther King, Jr.'s vision of a time when all will be judged by the content of their character rather than the color of their skin. That one mistreats the person against whom one discriminates explains the commonly held view that making hiring decisions on the basis of the color of an applicant's skin is impermissible. And if selecting employees based upon skin color is wrong, certainly selecting people to criminally dehumanize on that basis is at least equally so.

Perhaps a good way to capture this sentiment is to say that hate crimes are "senseless." Of course, no murder makes sense, but we are liable to lament Barry's act as particularly pointless. As depraved as Ally is for valuing $10,000 more than a person's life, Barry is worse because he regards the act of killing not as a means to some other end, but as an end in itself. He kills simply to indulge his irrational hatred, merely for the satisfaction of killing a Jewish person. Thus, without minimizing our disgust for Ally, there is plenty of room to regard Barry's state of mind as more vicious than Ally's. And, because retributivists assign punishments in accordance with the moral depravity of the criminal, Barry's more reprehensible state of mind explains why he deserves to be punished more strenuously than Ally.

Here, one might protest that hate criminals are not uniquely capable of intrinsically valuing killing: one can imagine a third murderer, Claudia, killing someone out of revenge (perhaps because the person hurt her child, had an affair with her partner, broke her heart, and so on), but it strikes me that Claudia's personal motive makes her mind less guilty than Barry's because of the absence of prejudicial discrimination. Of course, one could imagine a fourth murderer, call her Diane, who kills with neither a personal motive nor group animus [hatred]. But, someone like Diane, who randomly picks victims for the mere sake of killing, would not be a counterexample because most would readily concede that, if not insane, she is also especially depraved (even if her depravity is distinct from Barry's). In other words, while Diane is admittedly not a hate criminal, few would allege that it would be unjust to punish her more strenuously than typical murderers like Ally and Claudia. In the end, then, it seems as though a retributivist would recommend punishing hate criminals more strenuously because both their actus reus and their mens rea is worse than their generic criminal counterparts.

As the preceding analysis shows, any of the six theories can help explain the important moral aims that might be realized by punishing hate criminals more severely. If this is right, then we need not choose among the competing justifications for punishment to establish the desirability of imposing stiffer penalties for hate crimes.

4

Hate Speech Codes Will Not End Racism and Hate Crimes

Tim Wise

Tim Wise is an activist and lecturer against racism. He is the author of White Like Me: Reflections on Race from a Privileged Son *(2005) and* Affirmative Action: Racial Preference in Black and White *(2005).*

Hate speech codes have inflamed campuses for years, with impassioned advocates on both sides, but neither side is entirely convincing. Free speech absolutists ignore many restrictions on speech, such as libel laws and privacy regulations, and downplay the equal protection rights of people subjected to hateful speech and hostile environments. Advocates of hate speech codes, on the other hand, actually hinder the struggle against institutionalized, pervasive, and subtle forms of racism by focusing so intently on blatantly racist words and individuals. Everyone would benefit from more emphasis on meeting hateful speech with forceful anti-hate speech, ostracizing or even expelling bigots, and fighting for real diversity, rather than waging heated battles over abstract free speech rights.

As has been the case every year for as long as I can recall, an American college campus is once again embroiled in controversy over the expression of racism in its hallowed halls, and what it may seek to do in response.

This time the place is Bellarmine University, a Catholic college in Louisville, Kentucky, where, for the past several

Tim Wise, "Racism, Free Speech, and the College Campus," *Lip Magazine*, December 23, 2005. Reproduced by permission of the publisher and author.

months, freshman Andrei Chira has been sporting an arm-band for "Blood and Honour"—a British-based neo-Nazi and skinhead-affiliated musical movement, that calls for "white pride" and white power. Created originally as a magazine by Ian Stuart of the Hitler-friendly and openly fascist band, Skrewdriver, the Blood and Honour "movement" promotes bands that sing about racial cleansing and the deportation, if not extermination, of blacks and Jews. Blood and Honour's symbol, similar to the Nazi swastika, is that of the South African white supremacist movement, and is featured prominently on Chira's armband.

Chira, for his part, seems more confused than dangerous. All in the same breath he insists he is not a Nazi or neo-Nazi, but that he is a National Socialist (the term for which Nazi is shorthand). He insists he is not a white supremacist, a racist, or anti-Jewish, yet claims to be a supporter of the American National Socialist Movement (NSM), which calls for citizen-ship to be limited to those who are non-Jewish, heterosexual whites, and which group praises Hitler on its website.

All of which raises the larger question, which is not so much whether or not Chira should have the freedom to be an ignorant lout, but rather, how did someone so incapable of evincing even a modicum of intelligible (or merely internally consistent) thought, get admitted to a good college like Bel-larmine in the first place? Are there no standards anymore?

Is a Racist Symbol Free Speech?

Naturally, the debate has now begun to turn on the issue of free speech: Does the University have the right to sanction Chira or force him to remove the armband, or do his First Amendment rights trump concerns about the feelings of stu-dents of color, Jews (yes there are some at the Catholic school, both students and professors), and others who are made to feel unsafe by a neo-Nazi symbol?

It's a tug-of-war that has divided American higher education for years, with some schools passing restrictive codes limiting language or symbols that express open racial or religious hostility, and others taking a more hands-off approach. Bellarmine has remained uncommitted to any particular course of action. The University President has spoken in defense of Chira's free speech rights (and of the principle, more broadly), and has called for a committee to study the issue and determine what kind of policy the school should adopt to deal with hate speech.

To be honest, I have never found the main arguments of either the free speech absolutists or those who support hate speech restrictions to be particularly persuasive.

Buzz around campus has been split between free speech absolutists on the one hand (who seem to predominate), and those concerned about the way in which racist symbols might intimidate and further marginalize already isolated students, faculty and staff of color, on the other. Faculty have sniped at one another from both sides of the issue, as have students, and a group of about a dozen students launched a sit-in outside the office of the Vice-President for Student Affairs to insist on the inviolability of free speech rights. . . .

Having spoken recently at Bellarmine, and having met dozens of conscientious students and faculty there, concerned about addressing racism, I would like to take this opportunity to chime in, both regarding the existing free speech debate, and the larger (and I think more important) issue, which is how best to respond to racism, whether at a college or in society more broadly.

To be honest, I have never found the main arguments of either the free speech absolutists or those who support hate speech restrictions to be particularly persuasive.

The Problem with Labeling
All Speech as Free

On the one hand, the free speech folks ignore several examples of speech limitations that we live with everyday, and that most all would think legitimate. So, we are not free to slander others, to print libelous information about others, to engage in false advertising, to harass others, to print and disseminate personal information about others (such as their confidential medical or financial records), to engage in speech that seeks to further a criminal conspiracy, to speak in a way that creates a hostile work environment (as with sexual harassment), to engage in plagiarized speech, or to lie under oath by way of dishonest speech. In other words, First Amendment absolutism is not only inconsistent with Constitutional jurisprudence; it is also a moral and practical absurdity, as these and other legitimate limitations make fairly apparent.

Secondly, the free speech rights of racists, by definition, must be balanced against the equal protection rights of those targeted by said speech. If people have the right to be educated or employed in non-hostile environments (and the courts and common sense both suggest they do), and if these rights extend to both public and private institutions (and they do), then to favor the free speech rights of racists, over and above the right to equal protection for their targets, is to trample the latter for the sake of the former. In other words, there is always a balance that must be struck, and an argument can be made that certain kinds of racist speech create such a hostile and intimidating environment that certain limits would be not only acceptable, but *required*, as a prerequisite for equal protection of the laws, and equal opportunity.

So, for example, face-to-face racist invective could be restricted, as could racist speech that carried with it the implied threat of violence. Whether or not a neo-Nazi symbol of a movement that celebrates Adolph Hitler qualifies in that regard, is the issue to be resolved; but certainly it should not be seen as obvious that any and all speech is protected, just because of the right to free speech in the abstract.

Not to mention, does anyone honestly believe that Bellarmine, a Catholic school, would allow (or that most of the free speech absolutists would insist that they *should* allow) students to attend class with t-shirts that read: "Hey Pope Benedict: Kiss my pro-choice Catholic ass!" or "My priest molested me and all I got from my diocese was this lousy t-shirt?" No doubt such garments would be seen as disruptive, and precisely because they do not truly express a viewpoint or any substantive content, but rather, simply toss rhetorical grenades for the sake of shock value (likely part of Chira's motivation too).

Chira's armband, in that regard, is quite different from a research paper, dissertation, or even a speech given on a soapbox, or article written for his own newspaper, if he had one: namely, unlike these things, the armband is not a rebuttable argument, nor does it put forth a cogent position to which "more speech" can be the obvious solution. It provokes an emotional response only, and little else.

The Problem with Restricting Hate Speech

At the same time, the arguments of those who would move to ban hate speech have also typically fallen short of the mark, at least in my estimation.

Hate speech codes reinforce the common tendency to view racism on the purely individual level.

To begin with, speech codes have always seemed the easy way out: the least costly, most self-righteous, but ultimately least effective way to address racism. First, such codes only target, by necessity, the most blatant forms of racism—the overtly hateful, bigoted and hostile forms of speech embodied in slurs or perhaps neo-Nazi symbolism—while leaving in place, also by necessity, the legality of more nuanced, high-minded, and ultimately more dangerous forms of racism. So racist books like *The Bell Curve*, which argues that blacks are genetically inferior to whites and Asians, obviously would not be banned under hate speech codes (nor should they be), but those racists who were too stupid to couch their biases in big words and footnotes would be singled out for attention: in which case, we'd be punishing not racism, *per se* [for itself], or even racist speech, but merely the inarticulate expression of the same.

In turn, this kind of policy would then create a false sense of security, as institutions came to believe they had really done something important, even as slicker forms of racism remained popular and unaddressed. Furthermore, such policies would also reinforce the false and dangerous notion that racism is limited to the blatant forms being circumscribed by statute, or that racists are all obvious and open advocates of fascism, rather than the oftentimes professional, respectable, and destructive leaders of our institutions: politicians, cops, and bosses, among others.

Secondly, hate speech codes reinforce the common tendency to view racism on the purely individual level—as a personality problem in need of adjustment, or at least censure—as opposed to an institutional arrangement, whereby colleges, workplaces and society at large manifest racial inequity of treatment and opportunity, often without any bigotry whatsoever.

So, for example, racial inequity in the job market is perpetuated not only, or even mostly by overt racism—though that too is still far too common—but rather by way of the "old boy's networks," whereby mostly white, middle class and above, and male networks of friends, neighbors and associates pass along information about job openings to one another. And this they do, not because they seek to deliberately keep others out, but simply because those are the people they know, live around, and consider their friends. The result, of course, is that people of color and women of all colors remain locked out of full opportunity.

Likewise, students seeking to get into college are given standardized tests (bearing little relationship to academic ability), which are then used to determine in large measure where (or even *if*) they will go to college at all; this, despite the fact that these students have received profoundly unstandardized educations, have been exposed to unstandardized resources, unstandardized curricula, and have come from unstandardized and dramatically unequal backgrounds. As such, lower income students and students of color—who disproportionately come out on the short end of the resource stick—are prevented from obtaining true educational equity with their white and more affluent peers. And again, this would have nothing to do with overt bias, let alone the presence of neo-Nazis at the Educational Testing Service or in the admissions offices of any given school.

Hate Speech Codes Are a Distraction

In other words, by focusing on the overt and obvious forms of racism, hate speech codes distract us from the structural and institutional changes necessary to truly address racism and white supremacy as larger social phenomena. And while we could, in theory, both limit racist speech and respond to institutional racism, doing the former almost by definition takes so much energy (if for no other reason than the time it takes to defend the effort from Constitutional challenges), that getting around to the latter never seems to follow in practice. Not to mention, by passing hate speech codes, the dialogue about racism inevitably (as at Bellarmine) gets transformed into a discussion about free speech and censorship, thereby fundamentally altering the focus of our attentions, and making it all the less likely that our emphasis will be shifted back to the harder and more thoroughgoing work of addressing structural racial inequity.

Perhaps most importantly, even to the extent we seek to focus on the overt manifestations of racism, putting our emphasis on ways to limit speech implies that there aren't other ways to respond to overt bias that might be more effective and more creative, and engage members of the institution in a more thoroughgoing and important discussion about individual responsibilities to challenge bigotry.

So instead of banning racist armbands, how much better might it be to see hundreds of Bellarmine students donning their own come spring: armbands saying things like: "F. . . Nazism," "F. . . Racism," or, for that matter, "F. . . You, Andrei" (hey, free speech is free speech, after all).

That a lot of folks would be more offended by the word 'f . . . ,' both in this article and on an armband, than by the political message of Chira's wardrobe accessory, of course, says a lot about what's wrong in this culture, but that's a different column for a different day. The point here is that such messages would be a good way to test how committed people at Bellarmine really are to free speech, and would also send a strong message that racism will be met and challenged *en masse*, and not just via anonymous e-mails.

In other words, if Chira is free to make people of color uncomfortable, then others are sure as s. . . free to do the same to him and others like him. Otherwise, freedom of speech becomes solely a shield for members of majority groups to hide behind, every time they seek to bash others.

Creating an Anti-racist Culture Is the Solution

Instead of banning hate speech, how much better might it be if everyone at Bellarmine who insists that they don't agree with Chira, but only support his rights to free speech, isolated and ostracized him: refusing to speak to him, refusing to sit near him, refusing to associate with him in any way, shape or form. That too would be exercising free speech after all, since free speech also means the freedom not to speak, in this case, to a jackass like Andrei Chira.

Instead of banning hate speech, how much better might it be for Bellarmine University to institutionalize practices and policies intended to screen out fascist bottom-feeders like Chira in the first place? After all, Bellarmine, like any college can establish any number of requirements for students seeking to gain admission, or staff seeking to work at the school, or faculty desiring a teaching gig. In addition to scholarly credentials, why not require applicants—whether for student slots or jobs—to explain how they intend to further the cause of racial diversity and equity at Bellarmine?

And before I'm accused of advocating the larding up of the school's mission with politically correct platitudes, perhaps it would be worth noting that these values are already part of Bellarmine's Mission statement. To wit, the school's Mission statement, which reads:

> Bellarmine University is an independent, Catholic university in the public interest, serving the region, the nation and the world by providing an educational environment of academic excellence and respect for the intrinsic value and dignity of each person. We foster international awareness in undergraduate and graduate programs in the liberal arts and professional studies where talented, diverse persons of all faiths and many ages, nations and cultures develop the intellectual, moral and professional competencies for lifelong learning, leadership, service to others, careers, and responsible, values-based, caring lives. . . .

In other words, the school's entire purpose is consistent with the search for diversity and equity, and entirely inconsistent with the racism and Nazism of persons like Chira. So why shouldn't the school seek to ensure that only persons who adhere to, buy into, and are prepared to further the purpose of the institution itself, are admitted or hired to work there? Once there, individuals may indeed have free speech rights that protect even their most obnoxious of views, but that says nothing about the ability of the school to take steps that will make it much harder for such individuals to enter the institution to begin with.

Sadly, perhaps the most important missing ingredient in the struggle to uproot racism is white outrage.

Making a proven commitment to antiracist values a prerequisite for entry (and perhaps requiring some form of training in these issues or antiracist service project in order to graduate or receive tenure or promotion) would go far towards operationalizing the college's lofty (but thus far mostly impotent) mission, and would make controversies such as the present one far less frequent or relevant.

If Bellarmine is serious about stamping out racism, it is this kind of institutional change—which would both limit the presence of racists and increase the numbers of people of color and white antiracist allies, by definition—that they should adopt. No more platitudes, no more promises, and no more unnecessary debates about free speech. Create an antiracist culture from the get-go, by expanding affirmative action, diversifying the curricula, and using admissions and hiring criteria that sends a clear signal: namely, you may have free speech, but so do we; and we are exercising ours to tell you that you are not welcome here.

Why Are Whites Not Angrier?

Sadly, perhaps the most important missing ingredient in the struggle to uproot racism, is white outrage: not at those who challenge racism (oh we've plenty of anger for them, typically), but rather, at those who are white like us, and whose racism we listen to with amusement, more so than indignation.

So, for example, notice how the free speech supporters wax eloquent about the importance of upholding Chira's right to be a racist prick, but they evince almost no hostility towards [him] and his message, beyond the obligatory throwaway line: "I completely reject his views, but will fight for his right to express them." In other words, they are far more worked up about the possibility (however slight it appears to be) that the Administration may sanction the Nazi, than they are about the fact that *there is a Nazi on their campus in the first place.* Which brings up the question: does Nazism not bother them that much? Or have they confused the valid concept of free speech with the completely invalid notion that one shouldn't even condemn racists, out of some misplaced fealty to their rights (which notion of course relinquishes one's *own* right to speak back, and forcefully, to assholes like Chira)?

I long for the day when whites will get as angry at one of our number supporting bigotry and genocidal political movements, as we do at those who denounce the bigots and suggest that the right of students of color to be educated in a non-hostile environment is just as important as the right to spout putrid inanities.

What's more, I long for the day when whites stage sit-ins to demand a more diverse and equitable college environment for students of color (which currently is threatened by rollbacks of affirmative action, for example), just as quickly as we stage them to defend free speech for fascists, which, at Bellarmine at least, shows no signs of being endangered, so quick has the Administration been to defend Chira's liberties.

In the final analysis, when whites take it upon ourselves to make racists and Nazis like Chira feel unwelcome at our colleges and in our workplaces, by virtue of making clear our own views in opposition to them, all talk of hate speech codes will become superfluous. Where anti-racists are consistent, persistent, and uncompromising, and where anti-racist principles are woven into the fabric of our institutions, there will be no need to worry about people like Chira any longer.

5

Hate Crimes Legislation Criminalizes Thought

Don Feder

A nationally syndicated columnist, Don Feder is a staunch conservative and author of A Jewish Conservative Looks at Pagan America *and* Who's Afraid of the Religious Right? *He currently maintains his own Web site: Don Feder's Cold Steel Caucus Report.*

Hate crime laws are inherently unjust, inventing special classes of victims and creating a class of thought crime that violates the First Amendment. The impact of hate crimes is also vastly overstated, with almost one-half of so-called hate crimes involving verbal abuse alone. Indeed, Democrats cynically whip up hysteria about hate crimes in an effort to win votes and to paint Republicans as racists. In a time of real national danger, they are a useless distraction and in fact a threat to the rights we are fighting to protect.

After the Michael Skakel verdict [for murder of a neighbor], it can no longer be said that Kennedys (or Kennedy kin) can get away with murder. But they can still butcher the truth.

"Hate Crimes are terrorist acts. They are modern-day lynchings designed to intimidate and terrorize whole communities," [Democratic] Sen. Edward Kennedy hyperbolized on the Senate floor last June [2002].

Don Feder, "'Hate Crimes' Laws Would Criminalize Thought," *Human Events*, August 26, 2002. Copyright Human Events Publishing, Inc. August 26, 2002. All rights reserved. Reproduced by permission.

Kennedy was mightily miffed because the Senate tabled his bill to expand federal hate crimes law to include gender, disability and sexual orientation, so-called.

[Former] Senate Majority Leader Tom Daschle, (D.—S.D.), couldn't muster the 60 votes to cut off debate. Daschle decided at the last minute to try to stifle his colleagues. But, why waste time dispassionately discussing legislation designed to counter "modern-day lynchings?"

These Laws Are Illegitimate

In reality, hate crimes laws are an attempt at thought control.

The offenses covered—murder, assault, intimidation—are already crimes. The legislation seeks to increase penalties when they are motivated by bias. The extra punishment isn't for what the perpetrator did, but what he was thinking while he was doing it. It criminalizes beliefs.

Hate crimes also make a mockery of equality under the law by creating a dual standard of justice.

If you're battered, bruised and bleeding because your assailant has a personal grudge against you, the attacker gets one sentence. But if the same injuries are inflicted because of your race or religion (if Kennedy's legislation passes, add gender, disability or sexuality), the punishment is more stringent.

Except for a few fringe groups, comparable in size and effectiveness to the Flat Earth Society, there is no organized movement promoting hate crimes.

Is the generic victim hurt, humiliated or traumatized less than the target of group animus? If not, why is one crime more deserving of punishment than the other?

There Is No Real Threat from Hate Crimes

Returning to the September 11 analogy, Kennedy charged, "Republicans made it clear they will not take action to fight terrorism at home."

"Terrorism?" According to the FBI Uniform Crime Reports, nearly half of all hate crimes committed each year involve nothing more than verbal abuse. The World Trade Center victims would have been grateful if the hijackers had simply flown past the Twin Towers dragging a banner that read, "We Hate Americans!"

There is no epidemic of bias offenses in this country. The FBI report "Hate Crime Statistics 1997" notes that less that two-tenths of one percent of all aggravated assaults that year could be characterized as hate crimes.

Except for a few fringe groups, comparable in size and effectiveness to the Flat Earth Society, there is no organized movement promoting hate crimes. There are no training camps high in the Bavarian Alps, where skinheads are taught to taunt minorities.

There is no Axis of Hatred—no coalition of foreign powers actively promoting racist offenses in the United States. Aryan Nation poses no threat to our national security.

A Cynical Scheme

So, why the fuss? Why do Democrats insist that hate crimes are a danger to the republic comparable to Osama bin Laden or Saddam Hussein?

It's a cynical scheme to generate hysteria and harvest votes. By pushing these laws, Democrats tell minorities: "We're concerned about you. Those mean Republicans aren't. Little they care if you're the victim of a modern-day lynching."

With the credulous, this has paid off for them handsomely. In the last election, the sister of James Byrd Jr. (the black man who was dragged to death by racists in Texas) stumped for Vice President Al Gore.

Louvon Harris told a Philadelphia rally that George W. Bush, then governor of Texas, didn't think Byrd's murder was a "hate crime." (Harris supposed this from Bush's failure to support a hate crimes bill in Texas.)

Clearly, the three men who murdered Byrd (two are on death row, one is serving a life sentence—without benefit of a Texas hate crimes law) weren't motivated by deep affection and esteem. Bush and other hate-crimes skeptics, including dedicated civil libertarians, understand this.

But should feelings be criminalized? How you answer that question says nothing about your commitment to tolerance, but it speaks volumes about your regard for the First Amendment.

6

Hate Crimes Legislation Does Not Criminalize Thought

Dahlia Lithwick

Dahlia Lithwick is a senior editor at Slate, *an online magazine, and in 2001 she received the Online News Association's award for commentary. Her articles have also appeared in numerous print outlets, including the* New Republic, *the* Washington Post, *and the* Ottawa Citizen. *She is coauthor of* Me v. Everybody; Absurd Contracts for an Absurd World *(2003).*

There are obviously two sides to the hate crime debate, but in fact a third side has emerged and gained a lot of political clout. This side includes people who accept hate crimes laws in principle but strenuously object to extending the protections of these laws beyond race and religion. In particular, many religious people fear that attempts to include sexual orientation in hate crimes legislation would criminalize any assertion that homosexuality is wrong, leading to wholesale arrests of preachers and anyone else expressing this view. This is based on a profound misconception of the nature of hate crimes laws, which only come into force if an actual crime, such as assault or vandalism, has occurred. Mere speech is not criminalized. There are legitimate disagreements about hate crime legislation, but fearmongering based on ignorance is not helpful to that debate.

[In February 2005], the Montana legislature killed a bill that would have added crimes motivated by the victim's sexual orientation to the state's existing hate-crimes law. Opponents worried that such a provision would be used to target religious leaders preaching against homosexuality from their pulpits. Last week, a state lawmaker in Pennsylvania introduced legislation to remove language about sexual orientation from the state's hate-crime law—language first inserted only in 2002. His bill was inspired by the arrests of 11 evangelical protesters at a gay-pride festival [in Philadelphia] last fall [2004]. All charges were dismissed last week, but some of the defendants are now suing the prosecutors for bringing charges under Pennsylvania's hate-crimes or "ethnic intimidation" statute. And in Sweden, a pastor who'd been convicted under a broad national hate-crimes law for a sermon describing homosexuality as "something sick" and comparing it to pedophilia and bestiality was acquitted by an appeals court last week, which declared his words were protected by the country's free-speech laws. The Swedish hate-crime laws were amended to include homosexuals in 2003.

In the new push-me-pull-you of hate-crime legislation, gay-rights groups are winning victories by having crimes motivated by sexual orientation added to state laws, and conservative groups are just as quickly stripping it out based on constitutional claims of free speech and religion. There is a strange counterintuitive argument heating up across the land, based on the strange theory that it's not OK to hate based on race or religion, but that hating gays is somehow materially different.

The burgeoning new argument is that hate crimes against traditionally victimized groups are legitimate, but expanding their definition to include gays, women, or the disabled is not.

In 1981, the Anti-Defamation League released its model hate-crimes legislation, and 41 states and the District of Columbia have adopted similar laws, usually providing for enhanced sentences for hate-based crimes. (Arkansas, Georgia, Hawaii, Indiana, Kansas, New Mexico, South Carolina, and Wyoming have no hate-crime laws of any sort.) Twenty-four states currently include criminal acts based on sexual orientation in their statutes, as does the ADL model legislation. In 1990, the federal Hate Crimes Statistics Act was passed, requiring the Justice Department to collect statistics on all hate-motivated crimes. And Title 245 of Section 18 of the U.S. Code is the current federal hate-crime statute, allowing federal prosecution of hate crimes for intentional interference with the enjoyment of a federal right or benefit. Efforts to amend that statute in 1999 to include crimes based on gender, sexuality, and disability failed then and have every year since. The current statute punishes hate crimes based only on race, color, national origin, or religion.

Objections to Hate-crime Legislation

There are two main objections to these hate-crime statutes. The broad one is that, in general, a "hate crime" punishes mere speech or state of mind and is thus unconstitutional. This argument sweeps too broadly. No hate-crimes legislation targets constitutionally protected speech alone; that's why Bill O'Reilly [host of *The O'Reilly Factor*, a political-opinion television show] and Rush Limbaugh [a conservative commentator] still roam free. The basis of hate-crime legislation is the enhancement of penalties for conduct that is *already* criminal. Those Philadelphia [evangelical] protesters were arrested for refusing to obey police orders to relocate, not for the act of preaching itself. The U.S. Supreme Court agreed with this principle in 1993 with its unanimous decision in *Wisconsin v. Mitchell.* In *Mitchell,* the defendant was convicted of aggravated battery—a crime carrying a maximum sentence of two years. But the jury found he had intentionally selected his victim based on race, so his sentence was increased to seven years under Wisconsin's provision for hate crimes. The Supreme Court found that scheme constitutional, holding that "physical assault is not by any stretch of the imagination expressive conduct protected by the First Amendment."

The Orwellian notion that you can be jailed for your moral statements alone does not reflect the truth of the hate-crimes laws.

The burgeoning new argument is that hate crimes against traditionally victimized groups are legitimate, but expanding their definition to include gays, women, or the disabled is not. There are several interrelated ideas put forth by this latter camp. One is that women, gays, and the disabled were not historically and systemically singled out for abuse and oppression and so don't warrant special victim status under the law. Another is that there is no national epidemic of hate crimes against gays; this is an invention of the media. For instance, the FBI's Uniform Crime Reports study showed that in 1999 all hate crimes constituted less than one-tenth of 1 percent of criminal acts nationwide. Gay and lesbian groups counter with statistics suggesting that crimes against homosexuals are the third-most-prevalent type of hate crimes in the country. And the most ingenious new suggestion is that you can hate gayness without hating gays; that it's not persecution when you attack someone on the basis of sexual preference, it's merely an expression of your own religious freedom.

These new arguments for stripping sexual orientation from hate-crimes laws are conflations of all that is most wrong in the two classes of arguments above: They assume that non-criminal religious free speech would suddenly be swept up into the hate-crime net and that no religious person preaching that homosexuality is wrong would be safe. But unless there is an underlying criminal offense of "preaching" in this country, both claims are simply inaccurate. The free-speech laws regarding hateful speech are quite clear: Unless you are inciting your listeners to do imminent violence, your speech is pro-tected. The Orwellian notion that you can be jailed for your moral statements alone does not reflect the truth of the hate-crimes laws.

If we are going to debate whether gender, disability, or sexual preference should be added to state and federal hate-crimes legislation, let's have the rational, well-informed ver-sion of it. There are valid arguments on both sides. Slippery-slope arguments about wholesale jailings of the nation's clergy is mere fear-mongering, and debates over who's the biggest victim rarely result in fruitful policy.

The Problem of Hate Crimes Is Exaggerated

Dana D. Kelley

Dana D. Kelley is a writer from Jonesboro, Arkansas.

Despite a great deal of sensationalism, hate crimes are a tiny fraction of crimes, including violent crimes. In fact, lightning kills six times as many people each year as so-called hate crimes. While focusing so much on the miniscule problem of hate crimes, the media downplays the enormous prevalence of violent crime, which is a very real threat. The media should be much more responsible in putting hate crimes in perspective. In fact, we as a society should stop inventing false categories, such as hate crimes, and stay focused on reducing the overall crime rate, especially the dangerous prevalence of violent crimes.

The headline last Sunday [May 22, 2005] in the local Northeast Arkansas paper was a six-column screamer at the top of the page, right under the masthead where big news usually is announced.

Its five oversized words shouted out: "Area police investigate hate crimes."

From a headline of that dimension, it'd be fair to expect a volume of hate crimes larger than the bare minimum to create a plural noun. But the story recounted exactly two offenses, and one of them appeared to be as much a drunk crime as a hate crime.

Dana D. Kelley, "Crime Needs Context for Discernment," *Arkansas Democrat-Gazette,* May 25, 2005. Copyright © 2005 *Arkansas Democrat-Gazette.* Used with permission.

Even a stabbing and abduction on Wednesday got only a five-column headline.

Only when I turned to the paper's editorial page did I catch the smell, that unmistakable "rotten in Denmark" aroma that has often been slangfully described as simply "fishy."

In a typeface only slightly smaller than the front page's massive headline, the lead column read, "Differences, fear fuel hate crimes." The same reporter bylined on the front-page story also wrote the column. Together the stories basically amounted to a sermon on the ugliness of "hate," complete with the obligatory quotations from a "hate expert," in this case an editor from the Southern Poverty Law Center's anti-hate publication.

Journalists Should Avoid Sensationalizing Hate Crime

As a columnist, I fully understand the human desire to preach on issues of passion. But journalists must beware of sensationalism. The average reader who picked up that paper with its huge front-page headline would think this area [of Little Rock, Arkansas] had a hate-crime problem—which simply isn't true.

Ten inches down in the column, the writer openly acknowledges the truth: "Northeast Arkansas is no hotbed for hate crimes." No doubt he got confirmation on that from the Southern Poverty Law Center's Hate Groups Map, which clearly shows a clean slate in the northeast corner.

Near the end of the column the writer succumbs to the inevitable paradox that ultimately undermines all hate-crime reasoning: Hate is wrong except for hatred of the haters.

Violent Crimes Outnumber Hate Crimes

The double-barreled coverage left me wishing it had addressed crime in general, which is grossly underreported in analytical terms.

What crime needs today is context. The only explanation I can think of for our collective tolerance of an intolerably high violent crime rate is that our frame of reference has been corrupted, confused and obscured.

The hate-crime story actually provided a drop of context, if you could get through the bucket of sensationalism. It pointed out that across all 50 states and among 290 million people, there were only 7,500 hate crimes in 2003.

Compare that against 1.4 million violent crimes. You'll need a calculator to do the math, but it comes out to be more than 180 times as many. If you like percentage comparisons, that's 18,000 percent more violent crimes than hate crimes in a year. Perhaps the scarcity of official hate crimes explains why the SPLC's Hate Watch reports "incidents" rather than crimes.

It's hard to think of another instance in which a discrepancy of that magnitude results in the tiny issue getting more news play than the gargantuan one. Hate crimes resulted in only 14 murders in 2003, which is 300 times fewer than drownings, 1,400 times fewer than murders in general and nearly 3,000 times fewer than automobile accident fatalities.

We still consider lightning-strike deaths freak events, but they occur six times more frequently than hate-crime deaths.

The hate-crime "problem" in Arkansas is outpaced by violent crime at an annual rate of roughly 7,000 percent (170 hate crimes vs. 12,000 violent crimes). The real news of crime is that in just a couple of generations, the violent crime index per 100,000 people, which controls for population growth, has increased by a factor of four.

Hate Crime Is a Non-threat

Hate-crime sensationalism also muddies the water regarding racial dynamics. The threat that hate crime poses to the black community is literally nothing compared to the debilitating burden imposed on it by black-on-black crime.

High awareness of hate crime, basically a non-threat, only obscures the real threat. Worse yet, it obstructs discourse on real solutions.

Intellectually, hate crimes are not only non-threats but redundant misnomers. Any deliberate act of violent crime is the result of hateful emotions overriding respectful ones. Context in this area is dreadfully needed. The American public suffers from an inexplicable apathy regarding the pain victims suffer and the inadequate punishment violent criminals receive.

Whatever worry hate may warrant, worry more about crime.

Too often we simply don't stop to think about it. Movie violence, with its surround sound and dressed-up action gore, has crowded out the real thing in our minds. Some say we're numb to violence; I say we're not pricked nearly enough by it.

We've forgotten what it really feels like, and I believe that's one reason the violent crime rates have multiplied and never receded. In the 1950s and 1960s, adults were intimately acquainted with the violence of war, and it made them all the more intolerant of the cowardly violence of crime.

Context creates valid discernment. Next time you get a paper cut, imagine the pain of being slashed with a knife. Or if you bump your head hard, just imagine being struck full force by a strong criminal intent on robbing you. Remember your scariest childhood fright of someone "getting you," and then imagine it coming true like what has been happening with young children and sexual predators.

Nightmare crimes like those recur several thousand times a day. Whatever worry hate may warrant, worry more about crime. Much more.

8

Hate Crime in America Is Not Exaggerated

Brad Knickerbocker

Brad Knickerbocker is a reporter for the Christian Science Monitor. *In 1992 he was a corecipient of the Population Institute Global Media Award.*

Hate crimes are on the rise, and one reason might be a change in the national mood. War abroad and cultural war at home seem to be contributing to a national anxiety. Hate groups are proliferating on the Internet. At the same time, white supremacist organizations are splintering and radicalizing with the demise or imprisonment of their leaders. There is rising bigotry against Muslims, immigrants, and gay people. Minority groups are also attacking each other, with Latinos being responsible for the majority of racial hate crimes against African Americans, and vice versa. There is hope in some unusual and effective ways that communities are responding to hate crimes, and Congress seems to be taking the issue more seriously.

A recent spate of hate-related incidents around the country has raised a troubling question: Is there something about the mood in the U.S. today—perhaps spurred by Americans dying in combat abroad, plus the cultural and political war at home over issues like same-sex marriage, judgeships, and immigration—that is leading in some instances to threats and attacks?

Brad Knickerbocker, "National Acrimony and a Rise in Hate Crimes," *Christian Science Monitor*, June 3, 2005. Copyright © 2005 The Christian Science Publishing Society. All rights reserved. Reproduced by permission from *Christian Science Monitor* (www.csmonitor.com).

"Public discourse has become meaner and more cruel-spirited in general," says Mark Potok of the Southern Poverty Law Center (SPLC), who monitors hate groups and extremist activities in the US.

Recent incidents include cross burnings in North Carolina, threats against gay students on an Oregon campus, disruptions of anti-immigration meetings by those charging border vigilantes with racism, anti-Semitic graffiti in the Queens borough of New York, a whites-only group recruiting in Michigan, white separatists harassing Japanese residents in Las Vegas, and a rise in anti-Muslim activity.

Such trends can be difficult to gauge. States and localities use different definitions and reporting requirements. As the subject grows in public consciousness, incidents that may have gone unreported in the past now become known, giving the sense of an increasing problem.

But, says Chip Berlet, an analyst at Political Research Associates in Somerville, Mass., who specializes in hate groups and far-right activity, "I have seen what appears to be an increase in anger toward gay people and immigrants, as well as anti-Semitic conspiracy theories."

The Numbers

Among the quantifiable evidence:

- The number of active hate groups in the U.S. has grown from 474 in 1997 to 762 in 2004, according to the SPLC, and in the past four years the number of hate websites has risen from 366 to 468.

- The FBI reports more than 9,000 hate-crime victims in 2003 (the most recent reporting year). When an estimate of unreported crimes is added in, according to the SPLC, the total may be closer to 50,000 a year.

- The Council on American-Islamic Relations reports that civil rights abuses against Muslims rose 49 percent last year (to 1,522 incidents), and bias crimes committed against Muslims went up 52 percent. One example: Over the weekend, someone threw a rock through the glass door of a mosque at The Islamic School of Miami. Earlier in the year, a swastika and an obscenity were spray-painted on the school sign.

• Meanwhile, white-supremacist groups, experiencing the recent demise and disaffection of national leaders, are splintering, creating smaller and potentially more dangerous cells. Experts wonder whether this "leaderless resistance" (as radical right-wing theoreticians call for) will peter out or instead breed more "lone wolf" domestic terrorists—more Timothy McVeighs and Eric Rudolphs.

Minorities Also Commit Hate Crimes

While most hate crimes are directed against minorities, they increasingly involve minorities against one another.

Some see a parallel between Islamic terrorists led by Osama bin Laden and neo-Nazis, "Identity Christians," and other right-wing extremists linked to hate crimes.

In Los Angeles County, for example, most officially designated racial hate crimes directed against Latinos are charged to blacks, and vice versa.

"Whites don't have a monopoly on prejudice," says Brian Levin, director of the Center for the Study of Hate and Extremism at California State University, San Bernardino. "Different [racial and ethnic] groups now are rubbing elbows as populations grow"—bringing disputes over jobs, schools, and zoning.

Immigration, too, appears to be a major issue influencing relationships among racial and ethnic groups. There have been clashes between volunteer border monitors in the South-west and those who say such self-styled "vigilantes" encourage anti-immigrant bias.

Some see a parallel between Islamic terrorists led by Osama bin Laden and neo-Nazis, "Identity Christians," [Christian white supremacists] and other right-wing extremists linked to hate crimes. "Hating becomes a religious obligation," says Jean Rosenfeld, a researcher at the UCLA Center for the Study of Religion. "Demonizing the other is a precondition for killing and winning."

"This is the basic apocalyptic scenario," says Dr. Rosenfeld. "The enemy is God's enemy and evil. Eradicating the enemy is God's work and good. War cleanses the polluted world and prepares the ground for the advent of the millennial kingdom of peace and plenty."

For some, this has to do with race or religion. For others, it's homosexuality.

"The gay-marriage thing has freaked out those who see it as a sign of 'end days,'" says Randy Blazak, director of the Hate Crimes Research Network at Portland State University in Oregon.

Opponents Are "Evil"

The underlying conflict over such "values" issues in politics and society has sharpened the tone of public discourse, with opponents characterized as "evil" or "immoral" on talk radio or the Internet.

What's missing today, says Brian Levin of the Center for the Study of Hate and Extremism, "is the idea of democracy as compromise, as opposed to all-out victory at any cost." The result, he says, is a divided country and a lack of goodwill ex-emplified by personal attacks in politics and the media. In turn, that can lead to individual threats and assaults.

Around the country, communities are using traditional and unique ways to head off hateful situations.

In Bozeman, Mont., last month, a member of the white-separatist National Alliance who ran for the school board was trounced at the polls. Turnout was double last year's figures. "The community was incredibly offended by this guy," Martha Collins, a winning candidate, told the *Bozeman Daily Chronicle*.

And when a virulent gay-basher came to speak in San Francisco, those protesting his hateful rhetoric organized an AIDS charity fundraiser in which people pledged to donate so much for every minute he spoke. When the speaker found out he was inadvertently supporting those he opposed, he left.

In the US Senate, meanwhile, a bipartisan bill introduced last week would strengthen the enforcement and prosecution of hate crimes. A bill in the House would add protection based on sexual orientation, gender identity, gender, and disability to existing federal hate-crimes legislation addressing violent crimes.

9

Hate Crimes Against Muslims and Arabs Have Surged

Riad Z. Abdelkarim

Dr. Riad Abdelkarim is a physician and an activist on behalf of the rights of Arab Americans and Muslim Americans.

After the 9/11 attacks, there was a 1600 percent increase in hate crimes against Muslims and Americans who appeared to be of Arabic or South Asian descent, according the FBI. In fact, the FBI understated the problem, because of course it did not include incidents of harassment by police forces and government agencies, including the FBI itself. These were rather significant, especially for legal residents from so-called suspect countries, who found themselves targeted by the Immigration and Naturalization Services and often rounded up despite trying to conform to new regulations. Those who complied with the new "special registration order" from the Justice Department have seen their civil rights violated, which has only served to make Muslim communities more isolated and fearful of the government. This targeting of Muslims only serves to inflame already high tensions, and it has to stop.

For Arabs and Muslims living, working, and going to school in the United States, the end of 2002 and the beginning of 2003 were marked by poignant reminders of the unease and apprehension that has permeated their communities in the ongoing aftermath of the Sept. 11, 2001 terrorist attacks. First,

Riad Z. Abdelkarim, "Surge in Hate Crimes Followed by Official U.S. Targeting of Muslim, Arab Men," *Washington Report on Middle East Affairs*, vol. 22, April 2003, p. 51–52.

the FBI released its annual hate crimes report for 2001, which showed a marked increase in hate crimes targeting Muslims and people who are or appear to be of Middle Eastern or South Asian descent. Then, the INS [Immigration and Naturalization Service] announced a controversial new "special registration" process for non-immigrant visa holders from predominantly Muslim and Arab countries. That move rekindled concerns among these communities of unfair ethnic and religious profiling.

The FBI report found that incidents targeting people, institutions and businesses identified with the Islamic faith increased from a mere 28 in 2000 to 481 in 2001—a rise of 1,600 percent.

Although the statistics did not specify the dates on which the 481 incidents occurred, the FBI theorized in somewhat understated fashion that the increased attacks were "presumably . . . a result of the heinous incidents that occurred on Sept. 11." According to the report, most of the incidents against Muslims and people who are or were believed to be of Middle Eastern ethnicity involved assaults and intimidation. Three cases of murder or manslaughter and 35 cases of arson also were reported, however.

Unfortunately, as disturbing as these statistics are, the numbers of hate crimes reported by the FBI most likely vastly underestimate the true number of incidents that took place, as many Muslims are believed not to have reported such incidents to law enforcement authorities. According to statistics gathered by the Council on American-Islamic Relations (CAIR), a national Muslim civil rights and advocacy group, as of February 2002 the number of hate crimes and "anti-Muslim" incidents reported by American Muslims exceeded 1,700. These ranged from public harassment and hate mail to bomb threats, death threats, physical assault, property damage, and murder.

U.S. Government's Response

One question that has arisen in the aftermath of this surge in hate crimes is whether the U.S. government responded appropriately to the post-9/11 environment of anti-Muslim hysteria. The answer is both yes and no, according to a recently released report by Human Rights Watch (HRW), entitled *We Are Not the Enemy: Hate Crimes Against Arabs, Muslims, and Those Perceived to be Arab or Muslim After September 11.*

"Government officials didn't sit on their hands while Muslims and Arabs were attacked after Sept. 11," said Amardeep Singh, author of the report and U.S. Program researcher at Human Rights Watch. "But law enforcement and other government agencies should have been better prepared for this kind of onslaught."

The HRW report praises the official condemnation of hate crimes after Sept. 11 by public figures, including President George W. Bush. It notes, however, that "the U.S. government contradicted its anti-prejudice message by directing its anti-terrorism efforts—including secret immigration detention and FBI interviews of thousands of non-citizens—at Arabs and Muslims."

Indeed, after the initial wave of hate crimes against American Muslims and Arab-Americans, a second manifestation of the post-9/11 backlash ensued. Sadly, this backlash was in large part sanctioned by and carried out by our own government. It is interesting to note that one category of incidents compiled by CAIR—not to be found in the FBI report—is "FBI/Police/INS Intimidation," with a total of 224 reported cases. As HRW's Singh notes, "Since Sept. 11, a pall of suspicion has been cast over Arabs and Muslims in the United States. Public officials can help reduce bias violence against them by ensuring that the 'war against terrorism is focused on criminal behavior rather than whole communities.'"

Special Registration Program

This "pall of suspicion" has been extended further with the INS' controversial new "special registration" program, which overwhelmingly targets non-immigrant visa holders from Muslim and Arab countries. [Then-] Attorney General John Ashcroft initially announced the new program, the National Security Entry-Exit Registration System (NSEERS), in June 2002.

At that time, Ashcroft claimed the new program would "expand substantially America's scrutiny of those foreign visitors who may present an elevated national security risk." NSEERS requires non-immigrant visitors from countries deemed to be of "highest terrorism risk" to register with the U.S. government and be photographed and fingerprinted. The Justice Department estimated that between 100,000 to 200,000 visitors would be subject to the registration program.

Civil liberties groups, some members of Congress, and Arab and Muslim American groups immediately criticized the program, saying it singled out Muslims from Middle Eastern countries.

"It's pretty obvious that this plan won't work at anything except allowing the government to essentially pick on people who haven't done anything wrong but happen to come from the administration's idea of the wrong side of the global tracks," said Lucas Guttentag, director of the American Civil Liberties Union (ACLU) Immigrants' Rights Project. "Selective enforcement of any law based on unchangeable characteristics like race, ethnicity or national origin is at its core un-American."

An Eventful Date

The first registration deadline was Dec. 16, 2002, and targeted males aged 16 and over from Iran, Iraq, Syria, Libya and Sudan. That date did not pass uneventfully. In Southern California, hundreds of men and teenage boys were arrested at

INS offices as they voluntarily tried to comply with the new regulations. Many of these were Iranians—students, professionals, and others—as California is home to an estimated 600,000 Persians. Relatives who accompanied their male family members to INS offices in Southern California, expecting a 10- to 15-minute registration process as promised by the INS, instead left the offices sobbing and without their loved ones.

INS officials stated that those detained were held on immigration violation charges. Many of these had nearly completed the process for legal residency; others were in the midst of asylum or status adjustment applications. Although the Department of Justice and the INS refused to say how many people had been apprehended in California or around the country, estimates were as high as 1,000 in southern California alone. Some immediately posted bail and were released pending deportation hearings. Others, however, languished for days in crowded, unsanitary conditions where some claimed harsh treatment from authorities. . . .

A Warning from the Government

Later the same week, hundreds of community members attended an Orange County town hall meeting hosted by CAIR and cosponsored by other community organizations, where they heard such speakers as the wife of one detained man cry while she described her family's ordeal. Meanwhile Stephen Thom, a federal mediator with the Justice Department's Community Relations Service, was flown down from Sacramento to address the concerns of an increasingly angry Iranian-American community. His comments to about 40 community leaders are representative of the apparent intimidation tactics currently undertaken by the Justice Department. "I understand that there have been some demonstrations and some marches," Thom stated, then warned of the "negative effect" of such demonstrations. "It makes other people think you don't want to be here," he said. "I think we need to look at what is the impact of open, glaring challenges to our system."

The following week, four national organizations filed a class action lawsuit against Attorney General Ashcroft and immigration officials, asking for an injunction to prevent the INS from further detaining individuals in the process of applying for residency. The lawsuit was filed by the Arab-American Anti-Discrimination Committee (ADC), Alliance of Iranian-Americans, CAIR, and the National Council of Pakistani-Americans.

Amnesty International was especially concerned about the blatant racial profiling manifested by the targeted INS registration process.

"The effort to deport law-abiding people who could just as easily be allowed to continue the immigration process seriously undermines prospects for future compliance and constitutes an absurd waste of resources," the four groups said in a statement. "The mass arrests have further eroded confidence in the fairness of the INS and the immigration system among Arab and Muslim communities."

In a setback for those filing the suit, the Justice Department declared the following week that federal courts had no jurisdiction to review decisions carried out by the INS, with that power reserved only for the Supreme Court. . . .

Amnesty International Protests

Amnesty International (AI) eventually weighed in on the controversial registration process. In a letter sent to Attorney General Ashcroft on Jan. 10 (the second deadline date), AI "expressed concern" that NSEERS "could violate United Nations and international treaties to which the U.S. is party." AI's letter went on to call upon U.S. authorities "to review its immigration laws and procedures to ensure that they are administered in accordance with international law."

71

AI was especially concerned about the blatant racial profiling manifested by the targeted INS registration process. "Under international standards, targeting individuals on the basis of national origin is tantamount to racial discrimination," stated Dr. William F. Schulz, executive director of Amnesty International USA (AIUSA). "We are concerned that the INS, in requiring that nationals from specific countries submit to this process, is actively engaged in racial profiling."

These are troubled times indeed for American Muslims, Arab- and Iranian-Americans.

In its letter to Ashcroft, AI also noted that because the "special registration order applies only to immigrants from selected countries while similarly situated immigrants from other countries are not affected . . . this would appear to be in breach of the right to non-discrimination recognized under international law."

Benjamin Jealous of Amnesty's Domestic Human Rights Program commented on the irony that "those who fail to comply with the registration process face criminal charges and immediate expulsion—yet, in many cases, compliance has seemingly led to numerous rights violations. It is deeply disturbing that in the U.S., following the rules can lead to denial of legal counsel, food and necessary medicine or even to physical mistreatment."

Troubled Times

Despite widespread criticism of the special registration policy, the Justice Department and INS have shown no signs of abandoning the program, even leaving open the possibility that more countries might be added to the list in coming weeks. In the meantime, some of those due to register by spring have panicked, attempting to flee with their families to Canada. Asylum-seekers to Canada, however, have been rejected and sent back to the U.S., where out-of-status males have been detained by immigration officials upon their attempted return. As a result, entire families have been stranded in border towns, some living in their cars. In towns in Michigan, Vermont, and New York, desperate families have sought food and shelter as they await an uncertain future, many without their primary breadwinners.

These are troubled times indeed for American Muslims, Arab- and Iranian-Americans. . . . And the continued officially sanctioned harassment of Arabs and Muslims—citizens, immigrants, and students alike—by our own government through such policies as the INS special registration program and an array of other increasingly draconian [extremely harsh] tactics does little to alleviate the growing unease of American Muslims.

10

Hate Crimes Against Muslims and Arabs Have Not Increased

John Leo

John Leo is a contributing editor to U.S. News & World Report *and a syndicated columnist whose work appears in 140 newspapers around the country. He is the the author of* Two Steps Ahead of the Thought Police *and* How the Russians Invented Baseball and Other Essays of Enlightenment.

Despite fears after the 9/11 attacks, there has not been a sharp upsurge in hate crimes directed at Muslim Americans. That has not stopped some groups from inflating the numbers or trying in other ways to exaggerate the threat posed to Arab Americans and other Muslim citizens. This is because of the political power of assuming a stance as victims, a stance that can silence legitimate criticism and enhance a group's lobbying power in Congress. Unfortunately, this hate crimes fallacy and an obsession with condemning "racial profiling" has caused the country to avoid an honest conversation between Muslims and non-Muslims in America about the extent of the threat from Islamic extremism. Rather than embracing victim status, Muslims should face this threat within their own communities and help the rest of the country fight it.

The Council on American-Islamic Relations [CAIR] and other lobbying groups are reporting a rising tide of anti-Muslim bigotry and a massive increase in anti-Arab crime in America. Obvious questions: What rising tide? What massive increase?

John Leo, "Pushing the Bias Button," *U.S. News & World Report*, June 9, 2003. Copyright © 2003 U.S. News and World Report, L.P. All rights reserved. Reprinted with permission.

Former Los Angeles Mayor Richard Riordan, in an article he cowrote, says the reason we haven't heard or read about an upsurge in the crimes is that "by and large, the big backlash never occurred." There are incidents, a few of them horrible, and there are breathtakingly nasty comments, like the ones delivered by a few prominent evangelical preachers in the wake of 9/11. But there is no tide of hate crimes or bigotry because America decisively refused to scapegoat its Muslim and Arab citizens after 9/11 and is refusing to do so now.

The FBI reported 481 anti-Muslim incidents of varying seriousness in all of 2001. The media spun that number as huge. But why? All such incidents are deplorable, but the total doesn't seem large for a nation with 2 million to 7 million Muslims. The FBI's total of anti-Jewish incidents that year was more than twice the Muslim total.

Other bias numbers seem small, too. After conducting nearly 10,000 interviews with U.S.-based Iraqis earlier this year, the government reported opening only 36 cases of "backlash discrimination or hate crimes" in the entire United States. What we commonly get in incident reports is pessimistic rhetoric backed up by paltry or questionable numbers. The Muslim community "continues to be picked out and picked on," said the head of the Human Relations Commission in traditionally conservative Orange County, Calif. But his new stats show only 15 hate crimes and lesser incidents involving Middle Easterners and Muslims in all of 2002, compared with about seven a year during the 1990s. Orange County bigots who pick on Muslims are apparently not up to the job.

Activists Hyping the Numbers

Every now and then a Muslim spokesman slips and admits that the numbers aren't grave. When the executive director of the Muslim Public Affairs Council, Salam al-Marayati, testified before the California State Senate in May, he noted that fewer hate crimes against American Muslims were reported during this year's war in Iraq than during the 1991 Gulf War. Good news. But by the end of his testimony, he was back on message, claiming that "Anti-Muslim bias is a systemic disease of our culture today."

> *Officially, [the United States] is committed to the notion that a Swedish nun is as likely to set off a bomb as a young male visitor from Iran.*

Why do CAIR and other groups push the "bias" button so hard? Well, the victim stance works. It attracts press attention and has made the "bias against Muslims" article a staple of big-city dailies. It encourages Muslims to feel angry and non-Muslims to feel guilty. It raises a great deal of money, garners a lot of TV time, and gets the attention of Congress. And by pre-positioning all future criticism as bias, it tends to intimidate or silence even the most sensible critics. From a lobbying point of view, who would want to give up a set of advantages like this?

Missing an Opportunity

I have an answer right here: anybody who thinks the future is more important than strumming the same old bias guitar for several more years. The obsession with bigotry is delaying the honest discussion Muslims have to have with non-Muslims in America. Here's one conversational topic: In light of the threat from Islamist terrorists, what kind of heightened scrutiny of Muslims in America is appropriate and fair? By insisting that all such heightened scrutiny is illegitimate "racial profiling," the Muslim lobby and its allies have in effect banned rational discussion. In response, the government has opted for a broad policy of hypocrisy, denouncing racial profiling in public while encouraging it among workers who have the job of guarding against terrorism. Officially, it is committed to the notion that a Swedish nun is as likely to set off a bomb as a young male visitor from Iran.

Another important conversation, currently frozen by the bias issue, is the role of national identity. Many people around the world are downgrading their national identity and looking for supranational or subnational identities—like John Walker Lindh, the American Taliban [caught in Afghanistan fighting for the Taliban]. What is the impact of this trend on Muslims, who are historically more focused on a religious identity than a national one? And when Muslims abroad want to know how you feel about being both American and Muslim, what are you prepared to say? We notice that CAIR's new ad campaign, "Islam in America," has virtually nothing in it about living in America, feeling American, or sensibilities shared with people of other faiths and no faith. So how about it? Can we get beyond bias and talk about this?

11

Gay Marriage Is a Religious Hate Crime

Craige McMillan

Craige McMillan is a columnist for World Net Daily, *an online news site dedicated to upholding traditional values and exposing government corruption.*

So-called "gay marriage" is a threat not only to the age-old idea that marriage is a union between a man and woman. It is also a direct attack on religion and people of faith. Indeed the entire homosexual agenda is a threat. Homosexual activists are trying to use the courts and political power to force people to accept their deviant lifestyle. Such acceptance violates the rights of people of faith. In fact, it constitutes a kind of hate crime itself.

A lot has been lost in the debate about so-called "gay marriage." At the top of that list is the effect that redefining marriage will have on people of conscience and religious believers.

Marriage is an institution that has been present since the beginnings of recorded history. It has meant the union of a man and a woman, and provided within that union the stability necessary to create and nurture the next generation.

While not all such unions produce children, procreation is the reason that most governments give some special consideration in law and tax to marriage and the resulting family. No government that ignores the welfare of the next generation will long endure.

At least three of the world's major religions—Christianity, Judaism and Islam—condemn homosexual relations. These faiths prescribe varying degrees of punishment for those who practice such behavior. The most serious punishment is death.

The Effect on People of Faith

Amazingly, no one seems concerned about the effect that elevating such condemned behavior to the same position of dignity and honor that families receive will have on people of conscience and religious faith. We should expect homosexual activists to be one-sided and completely consumed with gaining cultural and legal sanction for their favored sexual pastime—that is the nature of the lust that consumes their minds and bodies.

The Catholic Church is a prime example. Even within the sacred confines of the priesthood, men were unable to control the lusts that ravaged their minds and bodies—and many, despite their stated intentions, ended up serving their lust by betraying the trust and innocence of those they sought to serve and lead to God. The result has been thousands of shattered lives among victims (and, one suspects, perpetrators as well).

We have a right to expect more than one-sided homosexual-advocacy from our judges, political leaders, pollsters and journalists. Yet our highest-ranking judges have betrayed their own oath to the Constitution to serve homosexual advocacy. They have cited international law over the Constitution in manufacturing a "right" to homosexual sodomy.

Throughout history, homosexuality has been characterized by uncontrolled lust.

Local political leaders who failed to reveal to voters their homosexual sympathies have brazenly ignored state laws restricting marriage to a man and a woman, and issued homosexual "marriage licenses," then conducted "marriage ceremonies" for the deluded "couples." Journalists have written about these incidents, yet never disclosed to their readers that they are homosexuals or supporters of the homosexual movement.

A Selfish Agenda

What do these people who advocate for their own unrestricted lusts imagine that people of conscience and faith are supposed to do if the activists accomplish their selfish, thoughtless agenda and mandate acceptance of their sexual lifestyle? Do they somehow imagine that their sexual proclivities should be rammed down the throats of the faithful, and God be damned?

Yes, they do. Witness the Boy Scouts. Little else would give homosexual activists or their supporters in government, media and academe more pleasure than forcing a Christian, Jewish or Muslim widow to rent her property to a pair of homosexual tenants in violation of her conscience, and in mockery of her faith. It is the barrel of the policeman's gun that they seek—and which they have now found in Canada, where it is illegal to speak against homosexuality. That the widow should have her property seized and turned over to homosexuals through the court system for denying them the legitimacy they crave is their end goal.

All that homosexuals have achieved since the 1960s has been achieved through manipulation, coercion or stealth.

Throughout history homosexuality has been characterized by uncontrolled lust. Today we see it in the "gay" personals ads, where men now advertise for sex with unprotected HIV-positive men. Nothing else, not even their life, matters. That is why homosexuals have historically been barred from government security service, military service and, yes, as Scoutmasters for Boy Scout troops. Has the Catholic Church not proven these concerns valid—in spades?

A History of Lies and Manipulation

All that homosexuals have "achieved" since the 1960s has been achieved through manipulation, coercion or stealth. In 1973, militant homosexuals invaded the American Psychiatric Association's annual meeting and disrupted the meeting to such an extent—threatening more the next year and the next and the next—that psychiatrists were bullied into removing homosexuality from their list of illnesses. By stealth, they invaded and crippled the Catholic Church's seminaries, and ultimately its parishes, destroying the lives of tens of thousands. Behind closed doors, homosexuality's adherents in government have hold closed meetings, excluding those who disagree with their plans. They then present their cherished goal—"homosexual marriage"—as a fait accompli.

It is not. Homosexuals are now fond of presenting their "struggle" as a "civil-rights struggle." That is a self-serving trivialization of what blacks, who had no control whatsoever over their skin color, suffered. Blacks did not suffer because their behavior was abhorrent or ill-considered, they suffered for marrying, having children and supporting their families in the workplace. Only someone whose lust had corrupted their mind and obscured all rational thought could believe otherwise.

America needs to make sure its politicians understand: You're not God, and the perversions you're peddling have no place in civilized society.

12

Religious Objection to Gays Is a Hate Crime

Arden Ranger

Arden Ranger is a poet and writer based in Oklahoma.

Hate crimes against gay people are getting more violent and apparently more premeditated. Behind this are a number of factors. The Internet has allowed hate groups to spread their message to a much wider audience. Laws such as the Defense of Marriage Act and the many bans on gay marriage lend an official legitimacy to homophobia. Most importantly, the influence of the religious right and their persistent campaign to demonize homosexuality make contempt and hatred for gay people acceptable to millions of people. In this atmosphere, hatemongers like Fred Phelps (of "God Hates Fags" fame) flourish and spread lies, such as the belief that homosexuals are mostly child molesters. This atmosphere of hatred is a big part of the problem, forcing gay people to live in fear and letting their persecutors feel justified in committing any kind of violence against them.

His name was James. In junior high and high school, he was a member of the chess club, played the French horn in the concert band, and was an average student and an exceptional friend. No matter what time of day or night, no matter why or where, James could be counted on to be there for his friends. After high school, James stayed in his hometown. He worked a regular job in an industrial town, did vol-

Arden Ranger, "Hate Crimes and Sexual Preference: How Extreme Fundamentalism Fuels Hate Crimes Against Gays," www.straightdope.com, June–July 2001. Copyright © 1996–2006 Chicago Reader, Inc. All rights reserved. Reproduced by permission.

unteer work at the hospital and was there when his friends needed him. On November 17, 1998, James was stabbed multiple times by two teens who discovered the one thing only James's friends had known: James Ward, the 6'5", gentle man whose shoulders were broad enough to carry his burdens and those of his friends, was gay. Three days later, his mother buried her oldest son next to her youngest son.

"Being right too soon is socially unacceptable." —Robert A. Heinlein

James's murder, like so many hate crimes against gays, didn't receive national attention like that of Matthew Shepard. It is only the most brutal ones that we hear about—the ones that cause the most sensation in the news. But every year, thousands are the victims of hate and bias assaults in this country and the numbers continue to rise. Moreover, it's not just the sheer numbers that are so alarming. It is the increased viciousness of the attacks that have many authorities and gay-rights groups concerned. No more are these attacks limited to name calling, vandalism and the occasional physical assault. Every year, more of these attacks end in the death or maiming of the victim, who, in more than a few cases, is merely perceived as gay by his attackers. Common are acts of intimidation, harassment, physical force or threat of physical force directed against the person, family and/or property, police abuse, vandalism, arson and murder.

Between 1991 and 1992, violence against gays rose 31%. The total number for 1997, . . . from the FBI [Federal Bureau of Investigation] Uniform Crime Report, was 1,102. While these numbers may not seem alarming to some, they are to the FBI, who report that for the first time since 1995, the number of reporting agencies has dropped. This is to be expected, since reporting isn't mandatory. New York, for instance, has 502 jurisdictions, but only 35 of them make reports to the FBI annually. This leads one to wonder just how many incidents are not represented in the final report. If we don't depend on agencies voluntarily reporting, there are other sources of information. According to the Associated Press newswire on 4/7/99, anti-gay attacks dropped 4% last year. A report by the National Coalition of Anti-Violence Programs, a volunteer organization with 26 community offices, showed the numbers dropped from 2,665 in 1997 to 2,552 in 1998. But before anyone could digest this, they continued to say that the attacks have been more aggressive and hateful, leading to more hospitalizations. The number of inpatient hospitalizations more than doubled, from 53 to 110. There was a 71% increase in assaults or attempted assaults with guns. Incidents involving bats, clubs and other blunt objects rose 41%. Unfortunately, police response, bias-crimes classifications, arrests and complaint processing, did not rise.

What does this all mean? It means that the perpetrators are getting bolder; actions are becoming more premeditated. As Richard Haymes, executive director of the [Anti-Violence] Project says, ". . . . you have to make a conscious decision to leave your home with a baseball bat."

Sources of Hatred

But what is the cause of these attacks? What is the source of all this hate? While the answers may be varied, we will look at three of what I believe are the largest contributors of the atmosphere of hate and intolerance that permeates any discussion on sexual orientation.

In less then three years, the number of active hate sites on the Internet increased from one to over 160. Typing "hate groups" into the Dogpile search engine yields over 7,000 results. The Internet, our window to the world, has become a new recruitment opportunity for groups that perpetrate hate. The worst are listed by Hate Watch, an organization committed to combating online bigotry, who maintain a list of "The Top Ten Hate Groups You Love to Hate." Among them:

- The American Guardian, a group "combating the Homosexual Agenda."

- Bob Enyart Live, who proudly proclaims that he was "born homophobic."

- Cyber Nationalist Group, whose members are not just against homosexuals, but apparently anybody who isn't them.

- The Christian Gallery; "The Creator's Rights Party" is committed to arresting "faggots of all types."

- S.T.R.A.I.G.H.T. (the Society To Remove All Immoral Godless Homosexual Trash)—their name says it all.

- RevWhite's Christian Politics, "World Faggotry Exposed!!"

That leaves the group that in my opinion is the most vile, GodHatesFags, the people from Westboro Baptist Church in Topeka who picket funerals of gays and AIDS victims. These are just a sampling of what you can find on the Net, with a little time. In a statement to Yahoo News on September 16, 1998, the Internet, according to Joe Roy, Director of the Intelligence Project and Poverty Law Center in Georgia, "Is the place where young people of the computer generation can vent their frustrations, exchange ideas, and download information to feed their hate."...

The Influence of the Religious Right

But it is the Religious Right that seems to be the most vocal, the most visible and the most persistent in their persecution of homosexuality that seems to be the biggest contributor. It isn't only the "quiet" condemnation from the likes of [conservative televangelist] Jerry Falwell that creates the cloud of intolerance. Although, much of the condemnation from the more mainstream pulpits mirrors the utterances of the extreme Right—or, as my friend Laymon refers to them, "The

Religious Reich." The only real difference is that one is more politically correct than the other. One uses "homosexual" where the other uses "fag." It is extremists, like Fred W. Phelps at the Westboro Baptist Church in Topeka, Kansas, who have set themselves up as the Almighty's judge, jury and executioner—though not directly. The church's Internet site, www .godhatesfags.com, contains what he maintains are biblical quotes that support his position, excerpts from legitimate publications such as *Newsweek* and the completely tasteless "Matthew Shepard has been in Hell for——days. Matthew's message from Hell." The link contains a picture of Matthew, surrounded by flames, with a screaming voice saying, "Listen to Phelps!" Also on the church's pages is a list of demonstrations attended and planned, as well as the sayings planned for their signs. Included are:

For the Shepard Funeral and Laramie Courthouse:

- Fag Matt in Hell

- No Tears for Queers

- God Hates Fags

- Fags Burn in Hell

- AIDS Cure Fags Imagine mourning the loss of your son while listening to those chants and seeing those signs.

Homosexuals are repelled by the implicit dishonesty of a church that welcomes them only if they keep their mouths shut.

When I compared the King James Version of the Bible verses Phelps claimed condemned homosexuals as "filthy, lawless, liars, murderers, and sinners before the Lord who doom all nations," I was not surprised to find that the verses Phelps called upon condemned general wickedness, murderers, thieves, but say nothing about anything resembling homosexuality to a reasonable person. . . .

Many believe that homosexual males are the majority of child molesters, despite study after study that finds the average child molester to be white, middle age, heterosexual and usually married. It usually follows that the same people who hold this belief to be true also believe that homosexuals "recruit." The followers of Phelps choose not to listen to the APA [American Psychiatric Association] claim that homosexuality isn't a disease or the latest claims by the medical community that it may not be a choice that's made, but a genetic predisposition. Instead, these organizations have found a place on Phelps's hit list. . . .

Hypocrisy of the Churches

Many churches let gays and lesbians give their tithes and worship, yet refuse to bless their unions. Homosexuals are repelled by the implicit dishonesty of a church that welcomes them only if they keep their mouths shut. Their communal self-esteem demands more of the institutional church.

For every statistic, there is one or more perpetrators who thinks what they are doing is sanctioned, if not by law, then by the very absence of a law protecting the victim.

"Why, with all the persecution, hate, and threats to my person would I choose to be gay?" Laymon Rupe asked in an interview with me April 26, 1999. "I have what I call the Red Shirt Analogy. Imagine that you live in a society that ruled that on, say, Thursday, anyone wearing a red shirt could be shot on sight, no questions asked. There would be no punishment for the offender. Who in their right mind, knowing that was the law of the land, would wear a red shirt on Thursday? You wouldn't even risk wearing a red t-shirt under your clothes, cause you'd know that anyone getting close enough to see it could kill you. Hell, I wouldn't even own a red shirt. That's what it's like to be gay. To be me."

According to the FBI Crime Statistics for 1997, over 59% of the perpetrators were white males, as in the murders of Matthew Shepard, James Ward and Billy Jack Gaither. According to news reports from ABC, *Newsweek* and the *El Dorado News-Times*, none of the defendants ever stands up and says, "I did it because he was gay." No, the usual defense, as in the aforementioned three cases is, "He hit on me. I felt threatened. I defended myself, justifiable homicide!" Intimidation is the most frequently reported hate crime offense. Murders, forcible rape, aggravated assault, simple assault and intimidation are the crimes against an individual tracked by the FBI. Forcible rape is less common than murder.

The numbers don't say it all. For every statistic, there is a person targeted for no other reason then their sexual orientation. For every statistic, there is one or more perpetrators who thinks what they are doing is sanctioned, if not by law, then by the very absence of a law protecting the victim, or because they believe they are doing "God's Work." For every statistic, there are friends and family who have to come to terms with the fact that someone hated their son, daughter, cousin, father, mother, sister, brother or valued friend for something they had no control over, hated them enough to pick up a weapon and kill them.

13

Hate Crimes Against Gays Are Exaggerated

Josie Appleton

Josie Appleton is a journalist published in numerous British newspapers and magazines, including the Times, *the* Guardian, *and the* Spectator. *She is a founding member of the Manifesto Club, an organization dedicated to bridging the left-right political divide in support of individual creativity and Enlightenment values.*

Despite the tragic murder of a gay man in London, the press is vastly overestimating the impact of homophobia. In fact, there is no evidence that antigay violence is increasing. The statistics used to prove this rise are highly misleading, since they include simple insults, graffiti, and even attacks on gay individuals by ex-partners or other gay people. They also include everyday crimes that happen to occur in places associated with gay people. Antigay prejudice still exists, but heavy-handed efforts to fight a mythical rise in homophobic violence may actually inspire the very bigotry they are designed to combat.

After the murder of a gay man, Jody Dobrowski, on Clapham Common [in London], there have been warnings about the rising tide of homophobia. An investigation in the [London] *Observer* reported 'a big increase in homophobic attacks', and warned that 'for many gay people harassment remains part of daily life'.

The murder was a tragic case. But how could anybody seriously claim that homophobia is on the rise?

Some seem to be forgetting that homosexuality was a criminal offence [in Britain] until 1967, and police would raid gay clubs and cart off their occupants. Former editor of *Gay Times*, Colin Richardson, was quoted in the *Observer* piece as saying: 'I can remember days when if the police were blazing their lights across Clapham Common, it was to intimidate the gay men who gather there. Now, it would be in pursuit of a case of violence against someone.'

Evidence Is Insubstantial

There is in fact no evidence that homophobic violence is on the rise. After the Clapham murder, there were reports of a 'spate of violent muggings' targeting gays on the Common—but this turned out to be two other incidents, one in mid-September and one earlier this month. Yes, homophobic hate crime has risen by 8.5 per cent in London over the past year. But the tally of 1246 incidents for 2004/5 isn't huge for a city of seven million people, especially given the nature of many of the incidents. The Metropolitan Police [Met] takes a broad-brush definition of homophobia, as: 'any incident, which is perceived to be homophobic by the victim or any other person (that is directed to impact upon those known or perceived to be lesbians, gay men, bisexual or transgender people).'

An analysis of homophobic incidents recorded by the Met in 2001 showed that the largest proportion—some 35 per cent for men, and 50 per cent for women—involved threats rather than violence; another fifth involved criminal damage or theft. As a Galop [a British gay rights organization] spokesperson told me, a threat could include 'somebody shouting "dyke" in the street', or graffiti insults on a wall: 'the police are interested in hearing about all of it. Graffiti should be taken very seriously.' And there were some odd anomalies in the Metropolitan Police stats: four per cent of the perpetrators were a partner or ex-partner, and some of the attacks involved sex. It seems that almost every incident against a gay person can be defined as homophobic.

While the police once raided gay clubs to arrest people, today they cruise them to encourage the reporting of hate crimes.

Straightforward crimes can also be classed as hate-crimes. Galop told me that it is handing on reports to the police of cases such as 'a man being robbed on a cruising ground', because this is about 'exploiting a weakness, a perception of gay men'. Meanwhile, a man being picked up at a bar and assaulted is apparently homophobic because 'sex is about power'.

The Effect of Greater Enforcement

While the police once raided gay clubs to arrest people, today they cruise them to encourage the reporting of hate crimes. In Merseyside there was a 133 per cent increase in homophobic hate crime between 2001 and 2004, mainly due to the hard work of its officers. A spokesperson for Merseyside police told me that initiatives include: 'A police surgery [meeting between police and community members] at a gay club every fortnight, to build relations between the police and the gay community'; 'meetings every three months at gay venues, to enable better access'; 'a self-reporting pack, so that you can report homophobic crime anonymously'; 'the Merseyside "Shoutline" where those who have been a victim of crime because of their sexuality can speak to someone, or report the crime, in confidence'.

While employers used to discriminate against gays, today they are called upon to serve their particular needs. In a Department for Trade and Industry-supported briefing paper, the gay rights organisation Stonewall warns employers about the hefty responsibilities they face in order to comply with new equal opportunities legislation. 'Almost every aspect of employment policy and practice throws up specific problems in relation to LGB [lesbian, gay and bisexual] people', it says. It recommends that employers set up gay 'networks' for their workers, for mutual support and ready recourse if discrimination occurs. And there are warnings about the pitfalls of 'indirect discrimination', which could even involve something like a free crèche: 'statistically [gays and lesbians] are less likely to have children than heterosexuals', ergo the crèche discriminates against them.

Prejudice Negligible in Most Cities

It is still uncomfortable to be the only gay in the village, but in cities where most gay people live, real prejudice is negligible. The police employs openly gay officers to work with the gay community, and one public face of the Metropolitan Police is the gay deputy assistant commissioner Brian Paddick. A [2004] Stonewall survey found that only 6.8 per cent of people expressed public prejudice against gays or lesbians, compared to 14 per cent against travellers or gypsies. Gay couples can walk hand-in-hand in many cities without drawing a second glance; they can invite their partners to works drinks without putting their job in jeopardy. Sporadic attacks do happen, but they are mercifully rare. And all this is to the good.

What isn't so good is the way in which gays and lesbians have become shock troops in the campaigns of the new elite. The promotion of the issue of homophobia by everybody from the Metropolitan Police to the Tory [Conservative] Party, and the supposed remedy of re-education, marks the changing of the political guard.

At a time when traditional institutions are suffering from something of an identity crisis, the gay issue is a shorthand way in which they can distance themselves from the past and show that they're 'with it'. Hence Tory Steven Norris' support for a gay museum in London, or the party's gay and lesbian summit for young people in March 2003.

This sexual correctness onslaught is far more likely to breed problems than is the gay couple living next door.

Features of gay culture that developed in backstreet ghettos and underground cellars, and expressed the community's marginalisation, are now celebrated across the board. Camp, as cultural critic Susan Sontag wrote in 1964, is a 'love of artifice and exaggeration'; camp is 'disengaged, depoliticised', and sees everything in inverted commas ('not a lamp, but a "lamp"'). Symbolised by the rise of Queen Graham Norton [a television personality], with [rock singer] Elton John as Queen Mother, camp has become chic in a culture that revels in irony, disguise and frivolity. Rather than gays getting out of the ghettos, everybody else wants to climb in to join them.

"Tolerance" Education Can Backfire

The new elite doesn't believe in much, but 'tolerance' is one of the few things it can hold to. According to its brand of illiberal liberalism, anything goes except for pariah views about sexuality or race. The campaign against homophobia is an attempt to discipline the public (particularly the white working-class male section of the public). One Stonewall publication [from 2004] on prejudice recommended that officials 'target marginalised areas of white majority society', explaining that 'young white unemployed men are more likely to act out their prejudices through violence'. Much was made of the skinheaded suspects in the Clapham case, and these were seen as the working-class rule rather than the exception.

The term 'homophobia' suggests an unnatural psychological perversion. While sufferers of arachnophobia might need forced exposure to spiders, homophobes apparently need exposure to the exuberances of gay culture—the 'gay and proud' marches, and initiatives such as the London gay museum, or London mayor Ken Livingstone's plan to educate the capital's schoolchildren about gay and lesbian lifestyles.

If there isn't so much prejudice now, there might well be once Livingstone has done his worst. This sexual correctness onslaught is far more likely to breed problems than is the gay couple living next door.

Whatever the changes for the better, there are new barriers to equality today. Gay rights organisations urge employers to make special allowances for gay workers, and cry homophobia every time a gay man has his mobile [cell phone] snatched. Instead of free and easy equality, gays and lesbians have become a drag act cheered on by the authorities.

14

Homophobia Is a Hate Crime

Dr. Omowale Akintunde

Dr. Omowale Akintunde is an associate professor of multicultural education in the Department of Teacher Education in the University of Southern Indiana. He serves on the editorial board of the Journal of the National Association of Multicultural Education. He has lectured widely and published numerous articles on education, race, and diversity.

The brutal murder of Matthew Shepard in 1998 should have been a wake-up call, an opportunity to rethink and reverse age-old bigotry against gay people in our communities, our schools, and our churches. Instead, hatred reasserted itself, and in fact homophobia has become a central item on the agenda of powerful leaders in the religious right. It is especially sad that so many black people, who should understand the huge cost of oppression, join in oppressing gay people. Part of the problem lies in the very words racism and homophobia. Rather than putting the blame on these abstract ideas, we should be fighting the individual racists and homophobes themselves. And as so often, those who remain silent or allow bigotry to flourish in their neighborhoods cannot escape blame when a violent hate crime actually happens. Speaking out against hatred and bigotry is everybody's responsibility.

Dear Matthew,

It has been 5 years since your body was found [lying] unconscious, brutally beaten and hanging from a wooden fence

Dr. Omowale Akintunde, "A Letter to Matthew," *Multicultural Perspectives*, vol. 6, 2004, pp. 49–52. Copyright © 2004 by Lawrence Erlbaum Associates, Inc. Reproduced by permission of Taylor & Francis Group, LLC, www.taylorand francis.com.

in Laramie, Wyoming. I wish that I could tell you that your death has caused a groundswell of opposition to homophobia. The truth of the matter is it has not. As educators, we are still afraid to even mention the word homosexuality in our classrooms much less promote the notion that homosexuals are normal and have that notion become a natural part of the curriculum. The word homosexual has become much like the word "nigger." No one ever dares to say the word "nigger," but despite their refusal to utter it, the word "nigger" continues to exist. No one seems to get that it is the fact that we can't say "nigger" that empowers that word, that gives it life and meaning. It is the fact that there is a word about me as a people group that is so utterly pugnacious that no one dares to say it. No one has made the connection, however, between a word so disdainful it can't be pronounced and being a member of the group for which that word describes.

I wish that I could tell you that after your death, the entire community coalesced, curricula were changed in the public schools, and that there was absolute fervor to implement a curriculum that promoted a liberatory pedagogy. But I would be lying. What happened instead was I looked out of my office window in McWhinnie Hall at the University of Wyoming one day and saw a group of Christians who came to campus carrying signs declaring that you were burning in hell and that you deserved to die.

They say that religion is the opiate of the masses; that being the case then, this new religious movement is not under the influence of opium, "crack" is the new drug of choice. I have never seen such hatred spewed in the name of invisible deities who have left such explicit instructions as who to hate. And, Matthew, gays are among the group the deity has left instructions to hate. So these religious zealots have made homophobia their agenda. But they are not just a group on a rampage. They have power. Because this nation is overwhelmingly Christian, they are able to transform their religious beliefs into cultural practice and governmental law. That is the power of dominant groups. We've seen this in other contexts before. In the racial context, the dominant group was able to convert its ideas, attitudes, and hatred for Blacks into centuries of chattel slavery. Because they were the dominant group, they were able to justify our slavery, profit from it, while people stood by and said nothing, they said God wanted this, too. It was our place as dictated by the Bible, that holiest of books which tells one who to love and who to hate. And thus they were able to translate their religious beliefs into social practice and governmental law.

In 2001, the Presbyterian Church and the National Baptist convention apologized for slavery 300 years after the institution was abolished. The Presbyterian church split over the issue of slavery and whether or not Blacks should be given the same rights as Whites and not be the property of White people. The Catholic Church tried to kill Galileo for saying that the earth revolved around the sun and not the other way around. They later apologized, too. You would think that these people would have learned from their mistakes. But it seems that 300 years is just enough time to forget the mistakes you made and repeat them again. The Episcopalian Church is now threatening to split over the issue of the ordination of a gay priest: same script, different cast.

In their groundbreaking article, "Coloring Epistemologies: Are Our Research Epistemologies Racially Based?," Scheurich and Young (1996) stated that "When any group—within a large, complex civilization—significantly dominates another group its construction of truth, morality, and reality not only become the dominant ways of that group, but also these ways become so deeply embedded that they are seen as 'natural' or appropriate norms rather than as historically evolved social constructions." Christianity has dominated our civilization for centuries. It is no longer religious belief: it is a cultural norm. That heterosexism is normal and gays are sick and abnormal is not just a belief. It is a cultural norm so deeply embedded in our cultural epistemologies, it is what we know when we don't know that that's what we know; children "know" homosexuals are sick and abnormal; it is taught on the playground, in our homes, our churches, our schools; it is in our skin, our pores, the air that we breathe; we are not fighting a prejudicial belief. Matthew—we are fighting a system, an institution, a culturally entrenched ideology, organized religion. God himself—even the President of the United States [George W. Bush] wants to alter our very Constitution to make sure that gays never ever have the rights of straight citizens. Parents cry when they learn their children are gay, kick them out of their homes. Children are committing suicide rather than live a life as a gay person. It is the unspeakable love, Matthew.

Christian Blacks and Homosexual Rights

I am particularly saddened at the response of many Blacks to homosexual rights, Matthew. Let me tell you three incidents in my life on which I now reflect. I want to tell you about Hillie. Hillie was the choir director at Revelation Baptist Church in Mobile, Alabama where I grew up. That choir under his directorship was renowned throughout a city where great Gospel choirs were the norm; no wedding, no funeral, no important religious rite was complete without Hillie singing. If I close my eyes and listen intently, I can hear him singing, Precious Lord, take my hand. . . .

The entire church loved him . . . until he died of AIDS. Not only did the church not grieve his death, the minister of the church refused to eulogize him or allow his body in Revelation Baptist. His response instead was one of the most hate-filled sermons I have ever heard about the horrors of homosexuality, and he said that Hillie had suffered the wrath of a God that despised him. I watched as large Black women in huge hats covered in silk and bows nodded their heads in concurrence. I decided at that moment that I would never succumb to such ideology again. I tried to organized a group of people to conduct a candlelight vigil outside the church in protest. No one wanted any part of it. In my "Issues in Multicultural Education" class, Matthew, we read, discussed, and critiqued an article by Michael D'Andrea (1999). In it, he discusses how he as a White man and all Whites in general are impacted by religious figures being portrayed as White people. He reasoned that if Jesus is portrayed as White, the mother of Jesus is portrayed as White, is it really such a leap, then, to deduce that God himself is White? He asserts that seeing Jesus portrayed as White gives Whites an inflated sense of ego and superiority and racial minorities an inflated sense of inferiority and internalized self-hatred. That day, as Reverend Taylor delivered his hate-filled sermon, I remember quite vividly the huge life-sized sculpture of Jesus, a White man nailed to a cross, hanging over his head. The implications are deep, Matthew. Really, really deep. Mel Gibson has just produced a movie about the life of Jesus. Of course, Jesus, the mother of Jesus and everyone in the movie are White people. People are flocking to see it in droves. It has become one of the highest grossing movies in the history of the medium. If what Michael D'Andrea says is true, then this movie must be a veritable feast for the White ego.

Later, as a teacher at Anacosta High School in Washington, DC, one of our students, Andrew, committed suicide. He had become so sick of the constant ridicule about him being gay that he could no longer take it. So he stuck his father's shotgun in his mouth and blew his head off. The next day at school as word of Andrew's death spread, the response by the students in our school was to throw a celebration party, so glad were they as one student put it, "the faggot is now dead." I watched in horror. This was an all Black school. When confronted, they all said God says homosexuals are wrong.

As Blacks, we were denied the right to vote, to marry members of the dominant group, to drink from their water fountains, urinate in their toilets. In World War II, my dad told me that even the military was segregated, and Blacks were not even allowed to die on the same battlefield as White people. Thus, while engaged in a war to free Jews from persecution, he was fighting in a war with fellow White soldiers who thought him too despicable to die beside them. Such hypocrisy is the nature of prejudice. But hypocrisy is the hallmark and the birthright of this nation. Thomas Jefferson, while drafting a declaration of Independence declaring that all men were created equal, owned slaves, and not even White women had the rights of the White male. To this day, there are teachers who are still afraid to teach these facts about Thomas Jefferson in their classrooms or refuse to do so.

The Difference between Homophobia and Homophobes

We are not fighting homophobia, Matthew. We are fighting homophobes. A lot of people don't seem to understand the importance of the distinction here. Let me explain it to you in another context. I was watching a PBS special recently based on the life of Dorothy Dandridge [the first African American to be nominated for the Academy Award for best actress]. The special provided an in-depth analysis of her life. Throughout the special, the narrator remarked as to how racism played a critical role in the negativity of her life and the life of Blacks in general. Because of racism, they said, Blacks couldn't vote; because of racism Blacks couldn't live in the same community as Whites; because of racism Blacks couldn't go to the same schools as Whites; because of racism Blacks couldn't use the same bathrooms as Whites; because of racism Blacks were completely cut off from and denied the same rights as Whites; because of racism Blacks couldn't marry Whites.

The Word "Racism" Is A Problem

At one point in the video, Matthew, the narrator told a story of an occasion when Dorothy Dandridge was performing at a hotel night club in Las Vegas. The narrator said that although Dorothy could go in the hotel to entertain White people, because of racism she couldn't actually stay in the hotel and use any of its facilities. That darn racism. The narrator said Dorothy balked and carried on until they eventually conceded to let her stay in the hotel but strictly forbade her to exit her room or to use any of the facilities. She asked if she could at least sit by the pool. She was informed that the hotel management said that if she were to so much as put her toe in the pool they would drain the entire pool. Why? Yes, you guessed it, Matthew: RACISM.

So, Dorothy being the revolutionary that she was, put her toe in the water in front of White people. Matthew, they drained the entire pool. The narrator said this terribly dehumanizing event took place because of racism.

Now, Matthew, I sat and I tried to picture that. You know, Dorothy in her bathing suit walking around that pool just dying to do something revolutionary and jump in that pool of water but then each time she tried to get in, I pictured a big blob of racism jumping in front of her and blocking her every effort. I pictured in my mind Dorothy jumping and running frantically trying to get around that big nasty blob of racism and get in the pool but racism kept jumping in front of her every time knocking her to the ground preventing her from getting in that pool. After all, the narrator said it was racism that prevented her from getting in the pool.

That's when I realized that that was how White people escaped being the reason why Dorothy Dandridge couldn't get in that pool, the reason why Blacks couldn't vote, use their toilets, attend their schools, marry their children. The way Whites got away with being [to] blame is because they shifted the blame to an abstract entity, RACISM—and as long as people fought racism, White people would continue the travesty. Racism didn't keep Dorothy out of that pool, Matthew.

White people did. White people made those rules and White people enforced them actively or passively.

Fighting Homophobes Instead of Homophobia

Now that's my point about what we are fighting here Matthew. We are fighting homophobia but we should be fighting homophobes. Homophobes are making the rules and enforcing them. Homophobes are sitting in state legislatures deciding that gays should not have equal rights; homophobes are attacking gays, killing them, slaughtering them like sheep, and hanging them from fences. And just like it wasn't racism that kept Dorothy out of that pool, it is not homophobia that is keeping gay people oppressed. WE are doing that Matthew. We are either doing it actively or passively. A lot of White people argue that although they were around in the fifties when Blacks were denied rights, they were not culpable because they weren't actually the ones who put up the colored signs and enforced the rules, they argue they didn't have voice. But that is a lie Matthew. They did have voice. But they said nothing. They may never have put a noose around a Black man's neck, but the violence of their silence was present at every lynching.

> *Homophobia did not kill you, Matthew; homophobes killed you.*

I suspect that most everyone will leave here today and resume their lives as usual. No one will leave here and demand that their children's curricula are altered to include homosexuals and the notion that homosexuals are normal; no one will stand up in their churches Sunday morning before that glorious White man nailed to a cross and declare that homosexuals are normal; no one will go home and form a community group and demand that homosexuals be afforded the same rights as straight people to include marriage and the right to openly live and love; no one will do that. I wish that I could tell you, Matthew, that the Blacks, the ones who have suffered the same persecution that you have, will leave this building and storm the White House outraged that the government is perpetrating the same openly institutional bias and hatred toward gays that they have to us. But they will not, Matthew. They will join the chorus of haters in the name of the God that has cursed them. You will matter least to the ones who have suffered most. We, who were declared three-fifths human in Article I, Section 2 of the U.S. Constitution. Ironic isn't it? Because you are like me, Matthew. You are the secret hate that no one publicly acknowledges, you are the thing that we all despise, hope our children don't become or marry.

You are the "N" word, Matthew, the love that dare not speak its name.

Speaking Out Is the Solution

Dr. King said that in the end, it will not be the hateful acts of the unrighteous that will be remembered but rather the righteous who sat by, watched unrighteous acts but said nothing. And that is why I am no longer afraid to speak out Matthew. Because my silence is complicity. Fifty years from now, when gays have full civil rights, and that day will come, Matthew, I do not want to say that I was there but I couldn't do anything about it. Because that is a lie, I am here and I can do something about it. Because we all contributed to your death. We may not have been there to beat you and hang you from that fence to die; but we were all there to lend a hand. We are continuing to contribute to the thousands of people who are beaten and commit suicide each year because they are gay. We help commit each gay murder when we don't cry out; we help commit each gay murder when we don't demand that schools teach a social justice curriculum that embraces homosexuals as people worthy of the same love and respect as straight people; we commit gay murder if we are not storming the court house doors demanding that gays be given the same rights as straight people. We want to exonerate ourselves like White people did when they blamed the actions of White people on racism, an abstract entity, Matthew, and blame your death on homophobia. We want to persecute the two boys who actually carried out the act and deny that we all have blood on our hands. Homophobia did not kill you, Matthew; homophobes killed you. And anyone who is not verbally demanding equal rights for gays and being absolutely unyielding on the issue is a homophobe.

I assure you that one day we will be ashamed that we had to vote on whether or not gay people should be treated as five-fifths human.

So, I am speaking out on your behalf because Dr. King is right. I am not concerned with what people will think about me today. I am concerned about how history will record my position. It is easy for us to look back at what we call the past and blame injustice on the ignorance of the times. But we can't see the ignorance of our own times. I assure you that one day we will be ashamed that we had to vote on whether or not gay people should be treated as five-fifths human. But as Dr. King said, it will not be the hateful acts of the unrighteous that will be remembered. We won't remember the Christian group that gathered on campus at the University of Wyoming after your murder with signs declaring you are burning in hell; we won't remember a President who called for a constitutional amendment to make sure that gays are not treated as if they are five-fifths human; we won't remember the preacher who stood in his pulpit and preached homophobia; we won't remember the school board or the teacher or the superintendent who fought vehemently against a social justice curriculum that advocated that all people, Black, White, Latino, gay, lesbian, Christian, Muslim, atheist, Buddhist are all equal to one another. What will be remembered, Matthew, are the people who sat by and watched injustice happen and said nothing.

I promise to speak out, Matthew. I hope all is well where you are now.

Sincerely Yours,
Omowale Akintunde

Organizations to Contact

The editors have compiled the following list of organizations concerned with the issues debated in this book. The descriptions are derived from materials provided by the organizations. All have publications or information available for interested readers. The list was compiled on the date of publication of the present volume; the information provided here may change. Be aware that many organizations take several weeks or longer to respond to inquiries, so allow as much time as possible.

American Civil Liberties Union (ACLU)
125 Broad Street, 18th Floor, New York, NY 10004
(212) 549-2500
Web site: www.aclu.org

Dedicated to the defense of the Bill of Rights and individual American liberties, the ACLU is often at the center of controversies concerning freedom of speech, separation of church and state, and the rights of the accused. Although initially opposed to federal hate crimes legislation because of its threat to constitutional liberties, the ACLU has endorsed particular bills crafted carefully to avoid impinging on free speech rights or attempt to outlaw bigoted beliefs. It generally opposed hate speech regulations. In addition to direct action in the courts and in Congress, the ACLU provides numerous educational materials and outreach programs for schools and for anyone interested in learning more about constitutional rights.

Anti-Defamation League (ADL)
823 United Nations Plaza, New York, NY 10017
(212) 867-8656
Web site: www.adl.org

The primary force beyond hate crimes legislation in the United States, the ADL has been fighting anti-Semitism and other forms of bigotry since 1913. Today it gathers and publishes information on extremist bigots, especially the growing number of hate groups on the Internet, and works with law enforcement and state officials to ensure implementation of hate crime statutes wherever appropriate. In addition, it provides legal and other services to Jewish organizations and communities to ensure their security and their rights.

B'nai B'rith International
2020 K Street NW, 7th Floor, Washington, DC 20006
(202) 857-6600
Web site: www.bnaibrith.org

One of the world's oldest Jewish rights organizations, B'nai B'rith has founded hospitals, orphanages, and numerous other charitable institutions throughout the world. In addition, it has taken on the enormous task of fighting bigotry in numerous nations through its many publications, museums, libraries, anti-hate programs, and direct lobbying of governments.

Cato Institute
1000 Massachusetts Ave. NW, Washington, DC 20001-5403
(202) 842-0200 • fax (202) 842-3490
Web site: www.cato.org

The Cato Institute is a libertarian public policy foundation dedicated to limiting the size and power of government and protecting individual liberties. As such, it opposes hate crimes legislation as a threat to the First Amendment and an illegitimate extension of government policing. Its publications include the *Cato Journal*, the *Cato Policy Report*, and *Regulation*, and numerous books, studies, and editorials.

Christian Coalition of America
PO Box 37030, Washington, DC 20013-7030 USA
(202) 479-6900 • fax (202) 479-4260
Web site: www.cc.org

Founded by Pat Robertson, the Coalition is a conservative Christian, grassroots organization devoted to electing like-minded people and to promoting legislation that enhances its view of social morality. It is opposed to hate crimes legislation generally and deeply opposes applying hate crimes legislation to sexual orientation, for fear that this would muzzle antigay rights commentators. In addition to lobbying Congress and the White House, it publishes voter guides to indicate where candidates stand on the issues it finds most important.

Council on American Islamic Relations (CAIR)
453 New Jersey Avenue SE, Washington, DC   20003-4034
(202) 488-8787 • fax (202) 488-0833
Web site: www.cair-net.org

CAIR is a grassroots civil rights organization dedicated to promoting greater understanding of Islam and in protecting the rights of Muslims in America. Its activities include voter registration drives, lobbying, mediation, and advocacy for those who feel their civil rights have been violated. It also publishes educational materials and compiles annual statistics on hate crimes and other forms of discrimination against Muslim Americans.

Federal Bureau of Investigation (FBI)
935 Pennsylvania Avenue NW, Washington, DC   20535-0001
(202) 324-3000
Web site: www.fbi.gov

The primary investigative arm of the U.S. Department of Justice, the FBI has numerous responsibilities in combating terrorism, counterintelligence against foreign agents, and investigating over two-hundred federal crimes, as well as providing support for state and local police forces as necessary. It is also responsible for compiling and publishing the annual Hate Crimes Statistics report, and it provides educational materials on hate crimes for teachers, students, and the general public.

First Amendment Center
1207 18th Ave. S., Nashville, TN   37212
(615) 727-1600 • fax (615) 727-1319
Web site: www.firstamendmentcenter.org

Affiliated with Vanderbilt University, the Center seeks to protect the First Amendment through educational materials and providing speakers for schools and conferences. It is also affiliated with the Freedom Forum, based in Arlington, Virginia, which is funding a "Newseum" dedicated to educating the public about the importance of free speech and press freedom. The First Amendment Center is opposed to hate speech codes as an infringement of free speech rights.

Foundation for Individual Rights in Education (FIRE)
601 Walnut Street, Suite 510, Philadelphia, PA   19106
(215) 717-3473 • fax (215) 717-3440
Web site: www.thefire.org

One of the most active organizations in opposing hate speech codes, FIRE operates both an Individual Rights Defense Program, which mediates and sometimes litigates disputes about student rights, and an Individual Rights Education Program, which works to inform the public about free speech and other rights on campus. Among numerous other materials, it publishes the *Guide to Free Speech on Campus* and *Spotlight: The Campus Freedom Resource.*

Hate Crimes Research Network (HCRN)
Department of Sociology, Portland State University
PO Box 751
Portland, OR   97207
(503) 725-3926 • fax (503) 725-3957
Web site: www.hatecrime.net

Based at Portland State University in Oregon, the HCRN attempts to link academic research on bias-motivated crimes by sociologists, criminologists, psychologists, and other experts. It hosts conferences, publishes books and papers, and provides an action guide to help individuals highlight the problem of hate crimes in society.

Human Rights Campaign (HRC)
1640 Rhode Island Ave. NW, Washington, DC 20036-3278
(202) 628-4160 • fax (202) 347-5323
Web site: www.hrc.org

The largest gay rights organization in the United States, the HRC is often at the center of controversies about the extension of hate crime provisions to gay, lesbian, bisexual, and transgendered people. Through its publications, lobbying efforts, campaign support for political allies, and outreach programs it promotes greater understanding of gay people, including highlighting the problem of violence and intimidation that has plagued numerous gay people.

National Association for the Advancement of Colored People (NAACP)
4805 Mt. Hope Drive, Baltimore, MD 21215
(877) 622-2798
Web site: www.naacp.org

For almost a hundred years, the NAACP has been fighting discrimination against African Americans at the ballot box, in the courthouse and legislatures, and through publications, educational outreach, and a host of programs. As such, it takes a strong interest in drawing attention to hate crimes and in vigorously prosecuting those who commit them to the fullest extent.

Simon Wiesenthal Center
1399 South Roxbury, Los Angeles, CA 90035
(310) 553-9036
Web site: www.wiesenthal.com

Founded by a Holocaust survivor who spent his life chronicling that horror and tracking down the perpetrators, the Center is one of the leading organizations monitoring anti-Semitic hate crimes throughout the world and neo-Nazi organizations. It also promotes greater understanding of Judaism, human rights, and the dangers of bigotry through its publications, its film division, Moriah Films, and its famed Museum of Tolerance, located in both New York City and Los Angeles.

Southern Poverty Law Center
400 Washington Avenue, Montgomery, AL 36104
(334) 956-8200
Web site: www.splcenter.org

The center, founded in Alabama in the midst of the civil rights movement, has long been a leading resource in monitoring hate groups. Its legal center fights all forms of discrimination, and its Intelligence Project closely tracks extremist organizations throughout the country. It also provides valuable information on the state of hate crimes laws and enforcement through its quarterly, *Intelligence Reports*, and through numerous books, articles, and Internet resources.

Tolerance.org
400 Washington Ave., Montgomery, AL 36104
(334) 956-8200 • fax: (334) 956-8488
Web site: www.tolerance.org

Operating primarily online, Tolerance.org provides educational materials, including some print materials, downloadable public service announcements, and outreach programs designed to help schools and communities understand and prevent bigotry, discrimination, and bias-related crimes. It also provides guidebooks to help both adults and minors become trained activists in fighting intolerance. It is affiliated with the Southern Poverty Law Center.

Bibliography

Books

Jeannine Bell   *Policing Hatred: Law Enforcement, Civil Rights, and Hate Crimes.* New York: New York University Press, 2002.

Anthony Cortese   *Opposing Hate Speech.* Westport, CT: Praeger, 2005.

Aladdin Elaasar   *Silent Victims: The Plight of Arab & Muslim Americans in Post 9/11 America.* Bloomington, IN: Authorhouse, 2004.

Katharine Gelber   *Speaking Back: The Free Speech Versus Hate Speech Debate.* Philadelphia: J. Benjamins Publishing, 2002.

Jon B. Gould   *Speak No Evil: The Triumph of Hate Speech Regulation.* Chicago: University of Chicago Press, 2005.

Nathan Hall   *Hate Crime.* Portland, OR: Willan, 2005.

Valerie Jenness   *Making Hate a Crime: From Social
and Ryken   Movement to Law Enforcement.* New
Grattet   York: Russell Sage, 2001.

Moises Kaufman   *The Laramie Project.* New York: Vintage, 2001.

Joyce King   *Hate Crime: The Story of a Dragging in Jasper, Texas.* New York: Pantheon, 2002.

Alan Charles Kors and Harvey A. Silverglate   *The Shadow University: The Betrayal of Liberty on America's Campuses.* New York: Harper, 1999.

Jack Levin   *The Violence of Hate: Confronting Racism, Anti-Semitism, and Other Forms of Bigotry.* Boston: Allyn & Bacon, 2007.

Jack Levin and Jack McDevitt   *Hate Crimes Revisited: America's War on Those Who Are Different.* Boulder, CO: Westview, 2000.

Barbara Perry   *In the Name of Hate.* New York: Routledge, 2001.

Daniel Pipes   *Militant Islam Reaches America.* New York: W.W. Norton, 2002.

Dina Temple-Raston   *A Death in Texas: A Story of Race, Murder, and a Small Town's Struggle for Redemption.* New York: Holt, 2002.

Alexander Tsesis   *Destructive Messages: How Hate Speech Paves the Way for Harmful Social Movements.* New York: New York University Press, 2002.

Periodicals

Steven Robert Allen   "Asking a Mexican," *Utne*, September–October 2006.

Anonymous	"Conflicts between Fundamental Rights," *Human Rights Quarterly*, August 2006.
Ian Buruma	"The Freedom to Offend," *New Republic*, September 4, 2006.
Tom Flynn	"The New Hate Speech," *Free Inquiry*, December 2006–January 2007.
Franklin Foer	"Moral Hazard: The Life of a Liberal Muslim," *New Republic*, November 18, 2002.
Janice M. Irvine	"Anti-Gay Politics on the Web," *Gay and Lesbian Review Worldwide*, January–February 2006.
Wendy Kaminer	"No Laughing Allowed," *Free Inquiry*, December 2006–January 2007.
Edward I. Koch and Rafael Medoff	"What Can Be Done about Holocaust Deniers?" *The Jerusalem Report*, January 8, 2007.
Mike McManus	"Growing Up with Phelps," *Advocate*, May 9, 2006.
David Luc Nguyen	"Hate Has Left the Building," *Advocate*, December 5, 2006.
Norman Oder	"Hate Speech Filters Draw Lawsuit," *Library Journal*, April 15, 2006.
Gary Pavela	"Only Speech Codes Should Be Censored," *Chronicle of Higher Education*, December 1, 2006.

Ziauddin Sarder	"Freedom of Speech Is Islamic, Too," *New Statesman*, February 13, 2006.
Pat Scales	"Free Speech," *School Library Journal*, June 2006.
Daniel Schorr	"Iran's Holocaust-Denial Conference: A Community of Hate," *Christian Science Monitor*, December 22, 2006.
Robert A. Sedler	"Speech Codes Are Still Dead," *Academe*, May–June 2006.
Joel Simon	"Of Hate and Genocide," *Columbia Journalism Review*, January–February 2006.
Andrew Sullivan	"What's So Bad About Hate?" *New York Times Magazine*, September 26, 1999.
James Traub	"Learning to Love to Hate," *New York Times Magazine*, October 26, 2003.

Internet Sources

Jim Burroway, "When Words Have Consequences: Hate Crimes and the Same-Sex Marriage Debate," *Box Turtle Bulletin*, January 30, 2006. www.boxturtlebulletin.com/Articles/000,007.htm.

Austin Cline, "Hate Crimes: Do They Punish Unpopular Speech, Thoughts?" About Agnosticism/Atheism, March 12, 2006. atheism.about.com/b/a/250171.htm.

David L. Hudson Jr. "Hate Speech & Campus Speech Codes," First Amendment Center, September 13, 2002. www.firstamendmentcenter.org/speech/pubcollege/topic.aspx?topic=campus_speech_codes.

Stephen Kinsella, "Hate Crime—Intentional Action and Motivations," Ludwig von Mises Institute, July 25, 2005. http://blog.mises.org/archives/003873.asp.

B.A. Robinson, "U.S. Hate Crimes: Ethical and Civil Rights Concerns," ReligiousTolerance.org, November 10, 2001. www.religioustolerance.org/hom_hat5.htm.

Index